EXCELLENCE!

– GOD'S QUALITY IN YOU

RANDY C. BRODHAGEN

EXCELLENCE!

Copyright © 2007 by Randy C. Brodhagen

ISBN: 0-9786581-3-2

Published by

LIFEBRIDGE
BOOKS
P.O. BOX 49428
CHARLOTTE, NC 28277

Printed in the United States of America.

Contents

Chapter 1

A Quality Plan For You

I have wonderful memories of our children growing up and can still remember when our son was small and I told him we were going to have to save some funds for what he was asking for. "Oh no, Dad," he replied, "All you have to do is go to the bank and they will give you the money!"

Oh, the joys of innocense! Since we had never discussed finances with him, he thought we could have everything we wanted.

Where did I get the idea that children shouldn't have to be fearful or anxious? The Lord tells us, *"...do not worry about your life, what you will eat; or about your body, what you will wear. Life is more than food, and the body more than clothes. Consider the ravens: They do not sow or reap, they have no storeroom or barn; yet God feeds them. And how much more valuable you are than birds! Who of you by worrying can add a single hour to his life?"* (Luke 12:22-25).

Some people have a tarnished understanding and relationship with the Lord. The often-used phrase "God helps those who help themselves" is nowhere to be found in the Bible, however, we are not supposed to be lazy and sit idly by doing nothing.

The Father shows and tells us what to do. He never suggests, "You'd better start worrying." Instead, He promises an abundant life. As David declared, *"I was young and now I am old, yet I have never seen the righteous forsaken or their children begging bread"* (Psalm 37:25).

NO DISAPPOINTMENT

Because of the close relationship I have with my Heavenly Father, I think of Him as my "Dad." Why do I say this? Because He loves me with an everlasting love which never changes or fades away.

Unfortunately, there are dads who have disappointed their children—even abusing or abandoning them. However, our Father never violates our trust.

In our physical existence, we have a veil of death to go through, however, in God's sight we go from *life to life.* Jesus declares, *"I am the resurrection and the life. He who believes in me will live, even though he dies; and whoever lives and believes in me will never die"* (John 11:25-26).

Think of it! There is no death with God—and no end

as we understand it in our finite minds.

When God said to Moses, "I AM WHO I AM" (Exodus 3:14), He was letting him know, "I am the existence. I am all that is. There is not anything which did not come from Me."

Personally, I don't want to leave
my Father's presence—because I have
an understanding of who He is.

AN ALL-KNOWING GOD

It may be disconcerting to many, but the Lord knows *everything.* One of His qualities is omniscience—the theological term for all-knowing.

We are each born with a natural curiosity and want to know what our tomorrow holds. Sadly, some people look for answers from the wrong source, including dabbling in the occult or demonic realm by consulting astrologers and fortune tellers.

The only thing the devil understands about the future is what's ahead for him—and us. He is headed for eternal destruction, but those who believe on Christ are going to be with the Lord forever. Satan doesn't like this, yet there's nothing he can do about his eventual sentence.

PLANS FOR A MEAL

When Jesus was preaching to a multitude of 5,000

and it was time to feed the hungry throng, He asked the disciples, *"Where shall we buy bread for these people to eat?"* (John 6:5).

This was a test—for Jesus already knew what He was going to do.

Philip answered him, *"Eight months' wages would not buy enough bread for each one to have a bite!"* (v.7). Then Andrew spoke up, *"Here is a boy with five small barley loaves and two small fish, but how far will they go among so many?"* (v.9).

Jesus didn't even bother to answer the question. After all, He had *invited* those people to eat and He never did anything without His Father's permission.

Lifting up the lad's lunch, Jesus said, "Thank You, Father, for this provision."And when the meager supply was passed out, it was our Heavenly Father who miraculously multiplied the loaves and fishes.

ADVANCE KNOWLEDGE

The plan of the Lord surpasses anything we can think or dream.

God informed Abraham what was going to happen with the children of Israel 400 years before it actually took place. He told him the people were going into the bondage of slavery, but God would send a deliverer.

He knew you before the foundation of the world was laid. The Lord knows every step of your life from beginning to end. As the psalmist expresses, *"For you created my inmost being; you knit me together in my mother's womb"* (Psalm 139:13).

God has a plan of provision waiting, regardless of your present circumstances.

Even if evil is intended, the Lord knows the devil's plans too.

Jesus said to Simon Peter, *"Satan has asked to sift you as wheat. But I have prayed for you, Simon, that your faith may not fail"* (Luke 22:31-32).

You may say, "Since Peter denied the Lord three times, his faith *did* fail." No. If you keep reading you'll find he came *back* to his faith.

Jesus knew Satan's intentions because His Father showed them to Him when He was praying.

We see this pattern throughout Scripture. God talked to Cain before he went to kill Abel. He asked, *"Why are you angry? Why is your face downcast? If you do what is right, will you not be accepted? But if you do not do what is right, sin is crouching at your door; it desires to have you, but you must master it"* (Genesis 4:6-7).

Yet, Cain didn't even listen. He disobeyed and took the life of his brother.

"I KNOW THE PLANS"

As a God of excellence and perfection, He cannot lie.

In the days of Jeremiah, false prophets were telling the people what they wanted to hear—"Get us out of captivity. We don't want to be in this place."

This was far from the truth. The Lord spoke through Jeremiah saying, *"Do not let the prophets and diviners among you deceive you. Do not listen to the dreams you encourage them to have. They are prophesying lies to you in my name. I have not sent them"* (Jeremiah 29:8-9).

The Father wanted the people to know, "You are going to be in exile here for years." Then He said, *"...seek the peace and prosperity of the city to which I have carried you into exile. Pray to the Lord for it, because if it prospers, you too will prosper"* (v.7).

God also promised, *"When seventy years are completed for Babylon, I will come to you and fulfill my gracious promise to bring you back to this place. For I know the plans I have for you...plans to prosper you and not to harm you, plans to give you hope and a future"* (vv.10-11).

The Father's path is carefully planned for our good!

THE KEY TO CONTENTMENT

The apostle Paul found the secret to a life of satisfaction and happiness. He said, *"I know what it is to be in need, and I know what it is to have plenty. I have learned the secret of being content in any and every situation, whether well fed or hungry, whether living in plenty or in want"* (Philippians 4:12).

Why could he say this? Because Paul's life was in his Father: *"For to me to live is Christ"* (Philippians 1:21 KJV).

Until people learn to be satisfied with what they have, they will never be content, no matter how much they accumulate. The Bible says, *"Whoever loves money never has money enough; whoever loves wealth is never satisfied with his income"* (Ecclesiastes 5:10).

Where there is no contentment, there is no lasting peace—the very thing the Father has come to bring.

Remember, God assures us, *"As I was with Moses, so I will be with you; I will never leave you nor forsake you"* Joshua 1:5).

Our Heavenly Father cares for us with an *everlasting* love. Even when we wander and stray off track, He still loves us and has a wonderful plan for our future.

Relax, knowing the Lord has provided exactly what you need. He doesn't ask you to bring one thing to the table because He knows you own nothing. *"'The silver is mine and the gold is mine,' declares the Lord Almighty"* (Haggai 2:8).

THE LORD'S CALENDAR

Your house, health, relationships and even the clothes

on your back belong to Him. You came into this world with nothing, and you are going to leave the exact same way. You could not even work if the Lord did not give you the ability and strength.

One of the amazing things about our Father in heaven is that He does not operate in a time frame as we understand it. Since He has no beginning and no end, there are no limits on Him. As Peter said, *"With the Lord a day is like a thousand years, and a thousand years are like a day"* (2 Peter 3:8).

WHAT MOVES GOD?

After a church service, a gentleman walked up to me and asked, "Pastor, what does it take to move God?"

I shared with him that since the Lord already knows everything about us, what He is looking for is our trust, contentment and complete faith in Him.

Throwing a tantrum, crying or complaining has no effect on Him. Personally, I doubt the Lord pays attention to prayers uttered from selfishness or out of our own lusts and desires.

God said to Joshua, *"Be strong and very courageous. Be careful to obey all the law my servant Moses gave you; do not turn from it to the right or to the left, that you may be successful wherever you go. Do not let this Book of the Law depart from your mouth; meditate on it day and night, so that you may be careful to do everything written in it. Then you will be prosperous and successful"* (Joshua 1:7-8).

The Lord is always ahead of you, preparing the way. When the scouts went into Canaan to discover what was in the land, God had already been there. All they did was confirm what the Lord had said; namely, it was a great place. Yes, there were obstacles, even giants, but the Almighty proclaimed, "It's yours!"

Friend, the first thing you need to know on your journey is that God has designed a path of excellence for you.

CHAPTER 2

THE EXCELLENCE OF HIS PRESENCE

Once, when I was talking with a man about the Lord, midway through the conversation I literally had to stop the exchange. Why? Because I was uncomfortable with the way he was speaking of my Father in heaven.

His comments were similar to the weak, pathetic teaching in some Christian communities which says God allows—or even *causes*—people to suffer. Since he was obviously headed down that path, I decided I was not going to sit there and listen to such unfounded drivel.

"Are you cutting me off?" the man asked.

I answered, "That's right." I became agitated because I know my Father has only good and perfect gifts for each of us. He is a good God who loves us deeply.

This particular individual was hostile as he talked about how the Lord disciplines His children. But I interrupted, "I suppose you teach your child not to go out in the street by backing over him with a car."

It was a harsh example, but I wanted to get his attention. I had an opportunity to share with him that when people step outside of the will and blessing of God, negative things happen, and people suffer. However, when they call upon the Lord, He restores, forgives, heals, delivers, and starts the rebuilding process to remove the consequences of what has occurred in their lives.

Finally, he started to get the drift of what I was talking about. When you discipline your children in love, it is just for the moment, then, after the correction is over, you show your affection for them.

By the time our conversation had ended, I was excited and thanking God because he was receiving the message.

WHO CAUSES SUFFERING?

In parting, I told the person, "I want you to look at the first chapter of the book of Job and see how Job got into trouble. In the beginning God had a hedge of protection around him, and no one could touch the man."

The devil had tried, but could not harm Job because of the Lord's shield of blessing.

God permitted the test, but Job contributed, tearing down the hedge himself with statements such as, *"That which I feared the most is that which came upon me.*

16

What I feared has come upon me; what I dreaded has happened to me" (Job 3:25).

The immature Job, said, *"The Lord gave and the Lord has taken away"* (Job 1:21) and *"Though he slay me, yet will I hope in him"* (Job 13:15).

Yet, it was not God's intention to kill Job.

The Lord was not the one causing the suffering; it was the devil's doing.

The Father only *allowed* Satan to test His servant (Job 1:8-12).

THE ABUNDANT LIFE

Jesus makes His purpose clear: *"The thief cometh not, but for to steal, and to kill, and to destroy: I am come that they might have life, and that they might have it more abundantly"* (John 10:10 KJV).

The Father in heaven brings abundant life because, *"...God so loved the world, that he gave his only begotten Son* [our Savior, Jesus], *that whosoever believeth in him should not perish, but have everlasting life"* (John 3:16 KJV).

The Lord also warns, *"... my people are destroyed from lack of knowledge"* (Hosea 4:6)—meaning they do not have the abundant life because of ignorance of who He is.

THE FOLLY OF UNBELIEF

In one of Jesus' parables, the man who buried the talents for which he was entrusted (Matthew 25), said to his master, "You are strict, harsh and cruel; I hid them because I didn't want to lose the money, thinking you might hurt me if I did."

What a pessimistic attitude! When people worry and fear, they are implying God is helpless. This is an affront to the Almighty.

To whom did the master then give the gift? He took it away from the one who buried the talent and gave it to the servant who had invested and accumulated the most.

Unbelief is an insult to God and, sadly, people who call themselves Christians often do not have a clue who their Father is. They act as if He has abandoned them.

In this society of broken homes, the Father wants us to know who He is and that He loves us. He sent Jesus to save our souls and mend our lives.

A MATTER OF CHOICE

We need to totally discard the "suffering for Christ" mentality. Nowhere in the Bible does it say we are to endure hurt and pain—except through persecution for our faith in the Word of God and our belief in the Lord.

Anguish, sickness, disease and poverty are part of the curse of the law (Deuteronomy 28). These evils came on people who did not believe on God and continued doing things their own way.

The disciples once asked if a certain man was born blind because either he or his parents had sinned. Jesus replied, *"Neither...but this happened so that the work of God might be displayed in his life"* (John 9:3).

When people look at the world condition, they question, "How could a kind and loving God allow all of this to go on?"

What is meant by the word "allow"? It means somebody chose the wrong path. All God does is permit the consequences since He gave us a free will.

***Because people have made the wrong
choices and yielded to their selfish desires,
it has cost them sorrow, suffering, heartache,
wasted time and money.***

Remember, the Lord says, *"This day...I have set before you life and death, blessings and curses. Now choose life, so that you and your children may live"* (Deuteronomy 30:19).

I am praying you make the right choice.

"GOD IN US"

In the last chapter we spoke of an all-knowing, omniscient God. He is also omnipresent—always present. The Lord is here!

I trust you will come to know our awesome Lord, so

you will never talk about Him in a negative way. Once you understand who God is, you will give every part of yourself over to Him and allow the Lord to fill you with His presence.

One of the great mysteries and *truths* of the Gospel is that of "God in us." Yet, when I look at the church and the people of faith around the world, I often see selfishness and self-centeredness. They live as if God does not exist. When problems occur, they complain and do not even acknowledge the Word which declares, *"God has chosen to make known...the glorious riches of this mystery, which is Christ in you, the hope of glory"* (Colossians 1:27).

Jesus promises, "If you believe in me, I will come and will be with you; I will bring the Father and the Holy Spirit." The fullness of the Godhead dwelt bodily in Him (Colossians 2:9).

TOTAL RESTORATION

When we rely on the Lord, understanding His presence is within us, even if we fail, through Him we can rise again.

The Bible tells us *"... all have sinned and fall short of the glory of God"* (Romans 3:23). Nevertheless, the Lord has given us the blood of Jesus to restore, heal, deliver and bring us back into His fullness. From the moment you say, "Jesus, forgive me," the glory of God returns and you are restored to His fellowship once more.

Space has no limits upon God because He is everywhere. It's not that He is *in* all those places, but He *is* all those places!

Everything in the entire universe operates with His hand resting upon it—under His control and jurisdiction.

THE ETERNAL BENEFITS

Let me share six reasons you need to stay in close communion with the Lord:

1. God's presence brings assurance.

There is comfort because the Lord is near. He says, *"I am with you and will watch over you wherever you go, and I will bring you back to this land. I will not leave you until I have done what I have promised you"* (Genesis 28:15).

Assurance of God's nearness is not determined by the size of the crowd. *"For where two or three come together in my name, there am I with them"* (Matthew 18:20).

2. God's presence brings protection..

The Lord gives you safety in the midst of trials. *"When you pass through the waters, I will be with you; and when you pass through the rivers, they will not sweep over you. When you walk through the fire, you will not be burned; the flames will not set you ablaze"* (Isaiah 43:2).

As the psalmist proclaims, *"God is our refuge and strength, an ever-present help in trouble"* (Psalm 46:1).

3. God's presences brings rest.

"The Lord is my shepherd, I shall not be in want. He makes me lie down in green pastures..." (Psalm 23:1-2).

The only time sheep are able to lie down is when they are totally secure and at peace— when they know all of the enemies and conditions of life are satisfied.

The Lord says, *"My Presence will go with you, and I will give you rest"* (Exodus 33:14).

4. God's presence gives us courage.

You're never outnumbered when the Lord is by your side. *"When you go to war against your enemies and see horses and chariots and an army greater than yours, do not be afraid of them, because the Lord your God, who brought you up out of Egypt, will be with you"* (Deuteronomy 20:1).

5. God's presence brings gladness and joy.

The Lord desires for us to be filled with Him to overflowing. He allows man to be happy in his days, *"...because God keeps him occupied with gladness of heart"* (Ecclesiastes 5:20). Even more, you will be able to say, *"You have made known to me the path of life; you will fill me with joy in your presence"* (Psalm 16:11).

The Lord once assured me, "In My presence are My presents." What marvelous gifts!

6. God's presence is forever.

The same Rock of Ages who was with Abraham, Isaac, Jacob, Moses, Daniel, Peter and Paul, is with you today. He says, *"... lo, I am with you alway, even unto the end of the world"* (Matthew 28:20 KJV).

You have the promise of eternity with Him.

CHERISH EVERY MOMENT

Our God is "immutable"— which means He does not change. The physical Jesus is ascended to heaven, but not the Son of God who is the same yesterday, today, and forever. He is the Lord of Hosts the Bible speaks of, and He, the Father and the Spirit are one.

Sit at His feet, listen to what He has to tell you and cherish every moment in His presence.

CHAPTER 3

YOUR SOURCE OF JUSTICE AND MERCY

There is a movement in the world today to completely exterminate the law of God.

However, this is not a new phenomenon. The apostle Paul dealt with those who said they were no longer bound legally by the commandments of the Almighty.

Throughout history, this has been the reason for nations to crumble—because it is God who causes nations to rise and to fall (Daniel 11).

When earthly governments operate according to the precepts and principles of the Creator, there is blessing. When they turn away from His law, the nations deteriorate from within—not from external armies. This is why Scripture tells us, *"Do not fret because of evil men or be envious of those who do wrong; for like the grass they will soon wither, like green plants they will soon die away"* (Psalm 37:1-2).

Those who do not come under God's mercy will face His day of justice and judgment. Paul tells us, *"Do not be deceived: God cannot be mocked. A man reaps what he sows"* (Galatians 6:7).

RIGHT AND WRONG

God's laws are not kept out of duty, rather from a heart which is yielded to Him. *"This is love for God: to obey his commands. And his commands are not burdensome"* (1 John 5:3).

The mandates of the Father are only grievous to the person who does not want to obey them.

Even *ignorance* of the law is no excuse. We need to find out what is right and wrong before God and before man—and the Lord has allowed us to have His Holy Word so we are able to determine the difference.

If He had not given us this information, He would not be a just God.

It is important that we as parents teach our children the ways of the Lord. When they are older, even if they should drift away, they are able to return because His mighty Word has power to change their lives and draw them once more into the things of God.

Understanding the Lord's quality of justice is vital.

SELFISH BY NATURE

What is happening in our culture is what was occurring when Paul wrote: *"There is no one righteous, not even one; there is no one who understands, no one who seeks God. All have turned away, they have together become worthless; there is no one who does good, not even one. Their throats are open graves; their tongues practice deceit. The poison of vipers is on their lips. Their mouths are full of cursing and bitterness. Their feet are swift to shed blood; ruin and misery mark their ways, and the way of peace they do not know. There is no fear of God before their eyes"* (Romans 3:11-18).

People are still selfish by nature and place themselves before anyone else. They want God out of their lives and would rather exist without rules or authority.

This attitude demonstrates a spirit of lawlessness which has been at work since Satan fell from heaven.

We know that *"Those who live according to the sinful nature have their minds set on what that nature desires"* (Romans 8:5).

What does God's Word say about the hour in which we live? *"There will be terrible times in the last days. People will be lovers of themselves, lovers of money, boastful, proud, abusive, disobedient to their parents, ungrateful, unholy, without love, unforgiving, slanderous, without self-control, brutal, not lovers of the good, treacherous, rash, conceited, lovers of pleasure rather than lovers of God—having a form of godliness but denying its power"* (2 Timothy 3:1-5).

There is a price to pay.

HIS NATURE AND ACTIONS

The two words used for God's justice in the Bible are "just" and "righteous." These terms are linked together and designate perfect agreement between God's nature and His acts. What He says is who He is.

As humans, our behavior mirrors what's going on inside. As Solomon wrote, *"For as he thinketh in his heart, so is he..."* (Proverbs 23:7 KJV).

God's quality of being *just* means who He is and what He does are the same. In other words, "What you see is what you get." There is no misrepresentation.

James tells us a double minded man is unstable in all his ways and cannot expect to receive anything from the Lord (James 1:7-8).

However, what God says is the same next week—or five thousand years from now.

WE ARE ACCOUNTABLE

"Just," doesn't necessarily mean "fair."

If you have ever been disciplined by the authorities for speeding, you may have thought it was unfair that the speed limit was 70 miles an hour. Yet the law is written because someone's life may be in jeopardy—including your own.

A person walking after the flesh thinks it is unfair

when he is told he cannot yield to his own temptations. But this does not mean it's not just.

Even though we live in a society where divine law is slowly being removed, God's commandments still stand.

No matter what we think, feel or do, we are accountable to our Maker—whether we believe in Him or not.

HIS RULES NEVER CHANGE

God's quality of justice indicates that *who God is* and *what He does* are exactly the same. Speaking about false prophets and deceitful people, Jesus said, *"By their fruit you will recognize them"* (Matthew 7:16).

Just because a mouse invades the cookie jar doesn't mean he is a cookie. Likewise, because somebody sits in church doesn't mean he is a Christian. You will know their belief by their behavior.

Being just, God establishes the way to life and peace. Consequently, He discerns what people do and say. The truth can only be as God sees it; otherwise what we have are opinions. Paul writes to the believers at Corinth, *"I care very little if I am judged by you or by any human court; indeed, I do not even judge myself. My conscience is clear, but that does not make me innocent. It is the*

Lord who judges me" (1 Corinthians 4:3-4).

Have you made rationalizations, justifications or excuses for your actions? The Bible says, *"Let your 'Yes' be yes, and your 'No,' no"* (James 5:12).

This is just. Ultimately we need to leave it to God to determine what is right and what is wrong.

Situation ethics has been taught in colleges for years. The concept behind it is that, depending on the circumstances, the rules change. Yet, God's precepts do not vary. His law is eternal, just, and holy

AN "EVERLASTING COVENANT"

The Almighty shows His loving favor to those who keep His commands. The Word tells us, *"... the Lord longs to be gracious to you; he rises to show you compassion. For the Lord is a God of justice. Blessed are all who wait for him! (Isaiah 30:18).*

You cannot say you love God and recklessly do your own thing. Otherwise you would be inconsistent and unstable.

The Father says: *"For I, the Lord, love justice; I hate robbery and iniquity. In my faithfulness, I will reward them and make an everlasting covenant with them. Their descendants will be known among the nations and their offspring among the peoples. All who see them will acknowledge that they are a people the Lord has blessed"* (Isaiah 61:8-9).

THE OBEDIENCE FACTOR

The movement to do away with the law of God in our land is thievery, because it is robbing people of His abundant life. It is also iniquity because it separates people from the Lord.

Regardless of what the world thinks, we must do things God's way, even though it will cause persecution. Jesus predicted, *"All men will hate you because of me, but he who stands firm to the end will be saved"* (Matthew 10:22).

God's eternal covenant is for those who live in obedience to His Word, submit themselves to Him and who refuse to defile themselves by the world's standards.

The Lord says we are to, *"Administer true justice; show mercy and compassion to one another"* (Zechariah 7:9).

Our Heavenly Father loves justice and mercy because they are truth as He sees it—and the truth will set you free.

HIS RIGHTEOUSNESS

Jesus went to the cross to take away the unjust things which have affected people's lives from the beginning of time. The blood of Jesus was given to cleanse and remove everything that separated us from God and to give us peace, joy and righteousness in the Holy Ghost.

Righteousness is a term which means right standing with God. That is why appropriating and applying the blood of Jesus is so important; without it, there is no life.

When His blood was deposited before the throne of heaven, it made us right with Him.

NO EXCUSES

We all stand accountable for our lives and actions—under His justice and mercy. But why do people continue to hide what is wrong and expect the Lord to bless them?

Here is the key: If we are faithful to *"...confess our sins, he is faithful and just and will forgive us our sins and purify us from all unrighteousness"* (1 John 1:9).

It is time for people to stand up and take responsibility for their actions. To say, "Oh, the devil made me do it," is a lame excuse.

Ask for forgiveness and settle the matter.

No one can stand and say, "I've done nothing wrong, and I'm perfect." Even the prophets of God in the Old Testament were subject to the Almighty.

The accusers quietly walked away when Jesus said, "Let him who is without sin cast the first stone." They were all guilty.

The Spirit of the Lord is calling us to accountability. We must be like David, who said, *"I acknowledged my sin to you and did not cover up my iniquity. I said, 'I will confess my transgressions to the Lord'—and you forgave the guilt of my sin"* (Psalm 32:5).

TRUE REPENTANCE

You will have no need to worry concerning the justice of God if you will repent before the Lord.

True penitence is not just saying, "I'm sorry." Rather, it is renouncing your wicked ways and turning to the Lord. *"...if my people, who are called by my name, will humble themselves and pray and seek my face and turn from their wicked ways, then will I hear from heaven and will forgive their sin and will heal their land"* (2 Chronicles 7:14).

If you have never asked Christ to come into your heart and forgive you of your sin, I am asking you to do so today. You can experience God's amazing love and mercy.

CHAPTER 4

WONDER WORKING POWER

Several years ago, when we were launching some new programs in our media ministry, the Lord showed me a vision. I saw a large kettle filled with an abundance of ingredients. It was simmering—and I could almost smell the inviting aroma.

Then, many hands reached out, trying to lift off the lid, but they couldn't. Next, I watched the hand of the Lord reach down as He easily removed the lid from the large kettle. Suddenly, everyone was able to enjoy a delicious meal.

The Lord was revealing to me that if we try to make things happen on our own merit, we will fail. Why? Because He will not allow man to take credit for what is His doing.

God was orchestrating the entire matter.

EVERYTHING IS POSSIBLE
The Lord operates in the realm of a quality called

omnipotence—which means He is an all-powerful God. Nevertheless, He makes us co-laborers, saying "Yoke up with Me, My way is easy" (Matthew 11:30). Plus, it produces results.

You can spend your life in frustration, trying to make something happen, but if your efforts are not in the Lord's divine plan, they are futile.

When Jesus walked the earth, there were people who demanded He perform miracles. Yet, the Lord never did anything for "show." His mighty works were always based on love and to meet a need. You see, *"God is not mocked; whatsoever a man soweth, that shall he also reap"*(Galatians 6:7 KJV)—for better or for worse.

The Lord rejects the power of man. He resists the proud and He gives grace and ability to the humble, to those who submit themselves to Him.

"'Not by might nor by power, but by my Spirit,' says the Lord Almighty" (Zecheriah 4:6)—which tells us things are going to happen when God is at work.

PHYSICAL WONDERS

It is awesome to know the Almighty created something out of nothing by simply speaking the Word (Genesis 1:3). He declares, *"I am the Lord, who has made all things, who alone stretched out the heavens, who spread out the earth by myself"* (Isaiah 44:24). This is significant since it means He did not need any assistance from us.

Actually, the Almighty helps those who *believe* Him. When they do, they are participating with Him and have a part in the power. He doesn't need our help, yet He allows us to be co-laborers in His Kingdom.

God not only created the world with His Word, it is how He sustains what He has made. As the writer of Hebrews states, *"The Son is the radiance of God's glory and the exact representation of His being, sustaining all things by his powerful word. After he had provided purification for sins, he sat down at the right hand of the Majesty in heaven"* (Hebrews 1:3).

If the power of the Almighty ceased, the whole universe would be in chaos in a matter of moments.

I am amused by people who worship the sun or the moon. Who was it that formed these spheres and set them into motion? Why worship creation when you have the Creator?

SPIRITUAL WONDERS

Just as God is at work in the physical world, He

performs spiritual wonders in our lives. *"For God, who said, 'Let light shine out of darkness,' made his light shine in our hearts to give us the light of the knowledge of the glory of God in the face of Christ"* (2 Corinthians 4:6).

When we are born again, God creates a miracle within us. We look in the mirror and see the same person, but a transformation has taken place on the inside. He makes His light shine and gives us the ability to recognize who He is; to receive His glory and to realize the purpose for our lives.

We are not just here to occupy time and space, get married, have kids and work till we retire. God has a specific plan and destiny for each of us, and when we understand this, there is a spiritual awakening.

Once we were dead to God, but now we are alive in Him. It is by grace—the ability of the Fathers' wonder working power—that we are saved through faith (Ephesians 2:8). It is His gift to us.

Before I met Christ, I had a mind, a body, a personality, an intellect, emotions and a will, but my spirit was dead. He caused it to come alive!

OUR CREATIVE FATHER

Think of the incredible power it took for God to come from heaven and make Himself a Man. It was by supernatural means since no earthly creature could ever do such a thing. Nor could man perform the mighty works of the Lord as shown through Jesus unless the Almighty is working through him. Finally, Christ was raised from the dead. Again, it was a supernatural act of God.

Today, as believers, we are alive because *He* is alive. Jesus came in the flesh, then ascended to take His place at the right hand of the Father. He is *"...able to do immeasurably more than all we ask or imagine, according to his power that is at work within us"* (Ephesians 3:20).

However, what we seek must be according to His will.

God's creative work did not end after the first six days. John the Baptist declared, *"And do not think you can say to yourselves, 'We have Abraham as our father.' I tell you that out of these stones God can raise up children for Abraham"* (Matthew 3:9).

When the disciples were praising the Lord on the road to Jerusalem for all the miracles they had seen, some of the Pharisees said to Jesus, "Rebuke your disciples!"

He replied, *"I tell you...if they keep quiet, the stones will cry out"* (Luke 19:40).

Yes, God has the power to create such praise.

"ASK WHATEVER YOU WISH"

There are many things we would like to accomplish, but we do not have the ability. Why? Because, *"A man can receive only what is given him from heaven"* (John 3:27).

Trying to carry the world's problems on our shoulders is foolish. We were not made to bear burdens, no matter how strong we are physically, mentally, or emotionally.

It does not matter how much money, fame or influence we have, we lack the power to accomplish the will or the purpose of God on our own.

Jesus says, *"...apart from me you can do nothing...*[but] *If you remain in me and my words remain in you, ask whatever you wish, and it will be given you. This is to my Father's glory"* (John 15:5,7-8).

Have you been discouraged because you have been trying to forge your own way? Say, "Forgive me, Lord. In Jesus' name, deliver me from myself—from those desires which are not according to your will and purpose."

The fact that only God can forgive and take away guilt is one more demonstration of His power in the spiritual and mental realms—and these affect the physical realm: "Which is it easier to say? Your sins are forgiven, or take up your bed and walk?" (Mark 2:9).

Many physical problems are caused by factors out of line in the spirit or mental realm. Only God's power can change this dynamic.

RECEIVING THE POWER

When our daughter was two years old, she had a terrible cough for several days—the kind that keeps you up all night!

As a concerned parent, I prayed, yet wondered why the Lord had not answered. "What is happening to my child?" I wanted to know.

Amazingly, the Father spoke to me, "Son, she likes being rocked."

What the Lord was telling me was that her desire to be held in the rocking chair was stronger than my own faith. I went to her and said, "Pumpkin, you don't have to be sick to be rocked."

"Okay, Dad" she replied.

The power of God went into my daughter, and two hours later she was up and running around, perfectly healthy. Finally, we could sleep well again!

THE FATHER OF NATIONS

God calls things that are *not* as though they *are*, and then they become (Romans 4:17).

For example, the Lord talked about Abraham as if he had a son even when the man was old and Sarah was barren.

Earlier, Ishmael was born of Abraham through Sarah's handmaiden, Hagar. But if you read the account and its aftermath, you know it was man's doing.

When God told Abraham that he and his wife would

have a son *together*, Sarah was hiding behind a curtain and thought nobody knew she was there. But she could not fool God. He saw her there, laughing, saying to herself, *"After I am worn out and my master is old, will I now have this pleasure?"* (Genesis 18:12).

Then God said to Abraham, *"Is anything too hard for the Lord? I will return to you at the appointed time next year and Sarah will have a son"* (v.14).

It happened just as the Lord told them—and Isaac was born.

> ### This was a supernatural birth—the product of God's power. Only the Almighty can make a barren woman conceive.

The prophecy came true that Abraham would indeed be the father of many nations.

TAKE CHARGE!

You cannot always live your life as a helpless, hopeless victim. There comes a time when you must operate with authority and power—which only comes from on high.

God asked Cain, *"Why are you angry? Why is your face downcast? If you do what is right, will you not be accepted? But if you do not do what is right, sin is crouching at your door; it desires to have you, but you must master it"* (Genesis 4:6-7).

The Lord was warning Cain, "Take power over evil!"

Put the words of Jesus into operation: *"I have given you authority to trample on snakes and scorpions and to overcome all the power of the enemy; nothing will harm you"* (Luke 10:19).

We must take control over desires, cravings, lust, thoughts and unbelief. Be like Paul, who declared, *"Everything is permissible for me—but I will not be mastered by anything"* (1 Corinthians 6:12).

Once you understand how to use what God has given, get ready for some incredible results.

CHAPTER 5

"GREATER THINGS SHALL YOU DO"

Many years ago, when the Lord first called me to a Spirit-led ministry, we were about to conduct an open-air meeting when the black clouds of a thunderstorm began rolling in. Before long I could feel the raindrops.

Immediately, I thought about the words of Jesus when He was out on a raging sea and said to the waters, "Peace be still!"

At the same time, another passage of Scripture came to my mind: *"I tell you the truth, anyone who has faith in me will do what I have been doing. He will do even greater things than these, because I am going to the Father. And I will do whatever you ask in my name, so that the Son may bring glory to the Father"* (John 14:12-13).

I thought "Okay," and began looking up at the storm. Then I exercised my faith and said, "In Jesus' name, peace be still."

Praise God! The rain stopped and we continued the meeting.

HOLY GROUND

The Lord is ready to respond to your spiritual expectation and belief—if you will step out on His promises and claim the answer.

He is ready to fill your home with healing and blessing when you are willing to receive.

If you and your family are constantly in poor health, raise the banner of God, and say, "This household belongs to the Lord, and, in the name of Jesus, we are not going to have this illness in our home any longer. The blood of Jesus covers us; this is holy ground, and we refuse to accept this any more."

Just because the years are turning on the calender does not mean your body has to fall apart. Moses lived to be 120 years old, *"...yet his eyes were not weak nor his strength gone"* (Deuteronomy 34:7). Even at this advanced age, he climbed a mountain that would exhaust most 18 year olds.

God is no respecter of persons. What He did for Moses, He can do for you.

If there are people in your life telling you, "Your hearing is getting worse," or " You're not walking quite as straight as you used to," tell them you've decided not to receive negative comments any longer. Consider them evil reports.

ENOUGH!

The reason some people cannot put any gusto into their words is because they do not believe they have what it takes to change a situation. However, there is no power shortage with God.

There comes a point where you have to stand up and declare, "Enough! In Jesus' name!"—knowing you have the authority.

It is much easier to roll over and accept a negative situation. However, you need to realize it is one thing for the devil to broadside you with a truck, but it is an entirely different matter if you lie down and let him back over you! You should not tolerate his bullying.

"CALL TO ME"

There are literally thousands of promises in God's Word—and many we have not acted upon because we do not know they are available. This is why the Bible says, *"Now to him who is able to do immeasurably more than all we ask or imagine, according to his power that is at work within us"* (Ephesians 3:20).

We need to stay grounded in the Word to find out what the Father is thinking.

The Lord is saying to you at this very moment, *"Call*

to me and I will answer you and tell you great and unsearchable things you do not know" (Jeremiah 33:3).

He is not always telling you to confide in a pastor, talk to your friend or a member of your family. He simply says, "Call to Me."

According to Jesus, you do not need to go to any other person to reach God. He didn't even ask the disciples to personally pray to Him.

Instead, Jesus says, *"...the Father will give you whatever you ask in my name"* (John 15:16).

You have a direct line to heaven!

HE CAME TO HIS SENSES

People ask me why so many wonderful Christians suffer terrible circumstances. The Bible says, *"Many are the afflictions of the righteous: but the Lord delivereth him out of them all"* (Psalm 34:19 KJV)

So the problem is not that negative things happen. The real trouble is that we stay embroiled in the turmoil and allow the situation to control us.

King Nebuchadnezzar made the wrong assumption that all he had become and everything he received was due to his own efforts. He set himself up as "King of the Universe" and called himself *Great* King Nebuchadnezzar.

One day God decided enough was enough. The king went out of his mind and began grazing like a cow in the field. Insanity struck him because he refused to acknowledge that God was the one who continually blessed his life (Daniel 4).

Even though he spent years in this condition, he finally came to his senses through God's loving kindness and mercy. Then the king made this statement: *"I, Nebuchadnezzar, raised my eyes toward heaven, and my sanity was restored. Then I praised the Most High; I honored and glorified him who lives forever. His dominion is an eternal dominion; his kingdom endures from generation to generation"* (Daniel 4:34).

Nebuchadnezzar had a dramatic revelation—and an instant realization. He finally understood who had the true power and authority. When his response was to praise God, the Almighty restored him to the throne.

WALK IN UNDERSTANDING

Most people have little knowledge of the Lord. They have only heard about Him. Job said, *"Surely I spoke of things I did not understand....My ears had heard of you but now my eyes have seen you. Therefore I despise myself and repent in dust and ashes"* (Job 41:3,5-6).

When you walk with God in understanding you will experience progressive blessing which grows from faith to faith, increase to increase, wisdom to wisdom and glory to glory.

47

"PROVE HIM?"

The principle we learn from the devil's encounter with Jesus in the wilderness is that there is no power for power's sake.

After the Lord had been fasting for 40 days, the devil tempted Him, saying, *"If you are the Son of God, tell these stones to become bread"* (Matthew 4:3).

He certainly had the ability to do just that because *"...God anointed Jesus of Nazareth with the Holy Spirit and power"* (Acts 10:38). However, Jesus did not choose to turn the rocks into bread since it was not the will of His Father. So He told the devil, *"It is written: 'Man does not live on bread alone, but on every word that comes from the mouth of God'"* (Matthew 4:4).

The only time the Lord asks us to "prove" Him is in regards to our giving. He says, *"Bring ye all the tithes into the storehouse, that there may be meat in mine house, and prove me now herewith, saith the Lord of hosts, if I will not open you the windows of heaven, and pour you out a blessing, that there shall not be room enough to receive it"* (Malachi 3:10 KJV).

When the Lord makes such a bold declaration, it is important, because everywhere else in the Word we are told, *"Ye shall not tempt the Lord your God"* (Deuteronomy 6:16 KJV).

Jesus used these same words in the wilderness to answer Satan (Matthew 4:7).

STAND STILL!

I hesitate to pray while people are crying. It is a sign of fear and helplessness. Instead, I encourage them to be still and settle down. Why? Because it is faith, not tears, which brings results.

As the Lord told the psalmist, *"Be still, and know that I am God"* (Psalm 46:10).

When it was time for harvest and there had been no rain, Samuel stood before the people and said, *"Now then, stand still and see this great thing the Lord is about to do before your eyes!"* (1 Samuel 12:16).

FAREWELL TO YESTERDAY

I've heard people say, "I'm not ready to make my peace with the Lord. First I have to take care of some issues in my past."

Why go there? All Jesus says is, "You must be born again." Yesterday is history. *"Therefore, if anyone is in Christ, he is a new creation; the old has gone, the new has come!"* (2 Corinthians 5:17).

If you keep stirring up all the mistakes you have made, you are allowing your past to have power over you.

By refusing to sever your past, you are being stubborn, rebellious and unbelieving.

Even if you have repeated the same mistake 1,022 times, with God's help you can break the cycle and move into the life the Lord has prepared just for you.

Let the revelation of God's Word lead to realization—then action.

REMEMBERED NO MORE

When you bring your past to the Lord, it is buried forever. God will *"...tread our sins underfoot and hurl all our iniquities into the depths of the sea"* (Micah 7:19). He says your *"...sins and lawless acts I will remember no more"* (Hebrews 10:17).

Submit yourself to God, get right with Him, and ask His forgiveness.

The reason the problems of the past have a tendency to return, is because you have left an open door to Satan. He then backs his truck up to your house and steals your blessing. It is time to say, "Lord, forgive me, cleanse me, and close every door to the devil."

"BEFORE AND AFTER"

Never overlook the authority and influence of your testimony.

If you are free from a sin or habit, tell others about your victory. Even though the Lord has forgiven your past, He may want you to share part of your experience to help lead others to Him. So don't be ashamed to declare, "This is how I used to be, but let me tell you how the Lord has changed my life."

Your "before and after" story will inject power into your witness.

The Father has lavished His love on you so that you can be His child. He has transformed your life—erasing your mistakes and giving you a hope for today and promise for tomorrow.

What He has done for you is only the beginning. "Greater things" are waiting just ahead.

CHAPTER 6

A NEW NATURE

Y ou can purchase the most luxurious automobile in the world, but if there is a hidden crack in the engine, get ready for some headaches.

Real quality is not measured by a beautiful paint job or fancy trim. Those are just cosmetic. You'd better investigate what is going on under the hood!

Spiritually, the Lord examines us the exact same way. The Bible tells us, *"Man looks at the outward appearance, but the Lord looks at the heart"* (1 Samuel 16:7).

NO OTHER HOPE

There is only one reason God sent Jesus to earth to live as a Man and to die on a cross. It was so His blood would cleanse your *heart* from the sin you were born with. Remember, because of Adam's iniquity in the garden of Eden, we are *all* sinners. The Word declares:

"For all have sinned, and come short of the glory of God" (Romans 3:23 KJV). Only your acceptance of Christ's sacrifice can provide forgiveness.

It is marvelous what God has provided, yet He is not going to do more than He has already done through His Son. Christ is not going back to the cross.

If people do not receive God's gift—on His terms—they have no other hope.

For those who draw near to God with their whole heart, He will work on their behalf. The Lord says, *"Because he loves me...I will rescue him; I will protect him, for he acknowledges my name. He will call upon me, and I will answer him; I will be with him in trouble, I will deliver him and honor him"* (Psalm 91:14-15).

God will faithfully fulfill every promise He has made.

"NEITHER HOT NOR COLD"

We live in a day of frivolity which has even crept into the Christian community. Many are half-hearted concerning their faith, lacking passion or intensity. And those who have the fire of God on their lives are called "radical" or "fanatical"—and often avoided.

Listen to these stern words of Jesus: *"I know your deeds, that you are neither cold nor hot. I wish you were either one or the other! So, because you are lukewarm—*

neither hot nor cold—I am about to spit you out of my mouth" (Revelation 3:15-16).

These are the people who do not receive what the Lord offers. The hardened individual says, "I don't believe. This Christianity is a bunch of garbage!"

But more dangerous are the lukewarm:

- They know God's ways, but are not walking in them.
- They have compromised, yet still wonder why they are not blessed.
- They are disobedient, rebellious and independent, dishonoring God and His representatives. Still, they can't understand why there is no progress in their lives.

We need to come before the Lord and humble ourselves, spending time with Him and restoring our relationship.

TOTAL CONFIDENCE

We can have the same confidence expressed by Jesus: *"Father, I know you hear me always"* (John 11:42).

It was not a concern to the Lord as to whether God could raise Lazarus from the dead, but it was an issue to those who did not have faith. The unbelieving woman said, "He stinks by now" (John 11:39). After being dead four days, his body was decaying.

They did not realize the Lord had another plan for Lazarus—to raise him back to life.

REMOVING THE GUILT

The Lord forgives your heart, yet He cannot make a wrong right. If you break a civil law, there is a permanent record. God's forgiveness doesn't say you never committed such an act.

Some people have the idea that when they pray, they can ask the Lord to take away the memory of a negative event. However, what has taken place is real, and God cannot go back and change what has happened.

What forgiveness *can* do is take away its power over you—and the spiritual consequences of the sin.

Your Heavenly Father removes the guilt, hatred and bitterness of whatever it was in your life which caused you to commit the offense.

If it was a generational curse passed down from grandma, to mom, to you, forgiveness breaks the curse so you have the power not to repeat the behavior.

Of course, the devil will try to bring back to remembrance thoughts concerning what happened. But in the name of Jesus, the "stinger" which was left is now removed and there is no more pain. This is how God's mighty power works.

THE PROBLEM OF SELF

Evil rears its ugly head from selfish desires of the heart we are born with, and results in a "me, me, me" mentality. Only through a salvation experience can that nature be broken. Unfortunately, many carry this "I" attitude over into their walk with God—and even though they are saved, still tend to lead selfish lives.

If the Lord would step into the room and say, "You can take My place for a day," what decisions would you make?

Many given such power would want to reek havoc and revenge on all those who have done them wrong? Or they would opt for a new car, a new house—and perhaps a new spouse!

These are the willful choices of a self-centered individual.

If you ask people to list what they call sin, they will likely include murder, adultery, homosexuality, gossip, lying or cheating. Yes, those are sins, yet the most prevalent transgressions among believers are issues of our mind and emotions—worry, fear, stress, and unbelief.

This is why the Lord desires to change us on the inside. Only a pure heart can solve the problems of behavior.

IT'S ABOUT HIM

The reason we can make right choices is because we

have a new nature. The Spirit of the Lord is *in* you, which gives you the authority do what is virtuous and honorable.

Evil was broken at the cross by the blood of Jesus. No longer are you a miserable, wretched sinner.

It's not about *you*; it is all about God and others. You *"Love the Lord your God with all your heart and with all your soul and with all your mind...* [and you] *Love your neighbor as yourself"* (Matthew 22:37, 39).

"LOOK AT US"

One afternoon, at about three o'clock, Peter and John were on their way to the Temple for the time of prayer. About the same hour, a man who was crippled from birth was being carried to the gate—the one called Beautiful—to beg from those entering the Temple courts.

When he saw Peter and John approaching, he asked for a handout. Scripture records, *"Peter looked straight at him, as did John. Then Peter said, 'Look at us!'"* (Acts 3:4).

The man lifted his head and looked at them, expecting a handout.

Then Peter said, *"Silver or gold I do not have, but what I have I give you. In the name of Jesus Christ of*

Nazareth, walk" (v.6).

He lifted the crippled man by the right hand and pulled him up— and instantly his feet and ankles became firm and strong.

The Bible says, *"He jumped to his feet and began to walk. Then he went with them into the temple courts, walking and jumping, and praising God"* (Acts 3:8).

When the people saw him dancing around, they recognized him as the man who had always begged at the Temple gate.

They were, *"...filled with wonder and amazement at what had happened to him"* (v.10).

TIMES OF REFRESHING

Exceedingly joyful, the man threw his arms around Peter and John—while people came running to see the miracle which had taken place.

As a result, Peter was able to address the congregation, telling them, *"Men of Israel, why does this surprise you? Why do you stare at us as if by our own power or godliness we had made this man walk?"* (v.12).

Peter then preached one of the most powerful messages you will find in the New Testament. He told them the same Jesus who they crucified had risen again—and they were witnesses! He said: *"Repent, then, and turn to God, so that your sins may be wiped out, that times of refreshing may come from the Lord"* (v.19).

An Overflowing Heart

After a lifetime of being helpless and dependant, begging for bread, the crippled man was now shouting for joy because everything had instantly changed.

He was not only healed physically, he was transformed inside—his heart was bursting with happiness.

I can still remember the words I used to repeat as a young boy in Sunday school: "I am Jesus' little lamb, ever glad at heart I am."

When the Lord arrives on the scene, He instills hope instead of despair, joy instead of sorrow.

We are told, *"If ye then be risen with Christ...Set your affection on things above, not on things on the earth"* (Colossians 3:1-2 KJV).

Just as the Lord can touch your natural body, He can transform your heart, soul and mind. Praise God! You can have a new nature!

CHAPTER 7

FROM PRESSURE TO POSSIBILITIES

I can still feel the lump rising in my throat as my car started sliding dangerously backwards down the off-ramp on an ice-covered freeway. As I tried to maneuver the vehicle, my heart was pounding overtime.

Then, just as my car was about to skid off the road and over a cliff, out of my spirit I cried the word, "Jesus!" at the top of my lungs. It wasn't coming from my head because my mind was telling me, "You are going to die! You are going to die!

In this life and death situation, thank God my spirit was in tune with heaven and I called on the Lord.

He heard my cry and stopped the car right in the middle of the slide. It was amazing!

Once my heart left my throat and settled back where it belonged, the Lord spoke, "Son, as long as you were doing your fancy driving techniques I couldn't help you, but when you called My name I was there."

There are those who were skeptical and said, "Randy, you were just lucky!"

No. As long as I was trying to bail myself out, I was in trouble. But when I called on the Lord, there was a divine intervention. And no doubting Thomas can convince me otherwise.

"THEY WERE TERRIFIED"

Every person alive is affected by the tension and stress of life—whether the source is a negative doctor's report, lack of finances, a shaky job situation or conflict in a relationship.

Those in Bible times also dealt with pressure. How would you like to have been in Moses' sandals when the Red Sea was ahead of you and Pharaoh's army was chasing the Israelites from behind? They looked around to see the Egyptian chariots, horsemen and troops headed straight for them.

Scripture records, *"They were terrified and cried out to the Lord"* (Exodus 14:10).

This was before God divided the waters so the children of Israel could safely cross on dry ground—and watch the pursuing army drown before their very eyes as the sea washed over them.

THE PROBLEM SOLVER

At a wedding feast at Cana in Galilee, Mary, the mother of Jesus, had a typical reaction when things started to go wrong. She turned to her Son and said, "You have help. They have run out of wine for the wedding reception!" Jesus looked at her and basically wondered why she was asking Him, saying, *"...why do you involve me?"* (John 2:4).

Mary, knowing in her heart that her Son could solve the problem at hand, said to the servants, *"Do whatever he tells you"* (v.5).

The pressure of the moment resulted in His first miracle—Jesus miraculously turned the water into wine.

This was the beginning of a wondrous ministry that caused the lame to walk and the blind to see. Yet, before each triumph there was usually some form of tension.

Once, the disciples were aboard a vessel on the sea when a storm suddenly arose. Concerned for their very lives, they woke Jesus up, saying, "Master, if you don't do something we're going to drown! The water is coming into the boat and the storm is raging!"

They asked Him, *"...don't you care if we drown?"* (Mark 4:38).

After Jesus rebuked the wind and calmed the waves, He turned to the disciples and asked, *"Why are you so afraid? Do you still have no faith?"* (v.40).

There was no need to panic. The Master of the Seas

was with them.

OUR DELIVERER

The apostle Paul certainly knew what it was to endure stress. He wrote to the believers at Corinth, *"We do not want you to be uninformed, brothers, about the hardships we suffered in the province of Asia. We were under great pressure, far beyond our ability to endure, so that we despaired even of life"* (2 Corinthians 1:8).

Paul described how *"in our hearts we felt the sentence of death"* (v.9).

However, there is always a purpose in what the Lord allows us to experience. He writes, *"But this happened that we might not rely on ourselves but on God, who raises the dead. He has delivered us from such a deadly peril...On him we have set our hope that he will continue to deliver us, as you help us by your prayers"* (vv.9-11).

Yes, during our time on earth there will be pressure. But, thank God, there will always be a Provider.

MUSTARD-SEED FAITH

The excellence of the Father is demonstrated by the exercise of His will—not just over physical matters, but in hearts and lives.

When Jesus descended from the mount of Transfiguration, a man approached and knelt before Him, saying, *"Lord, have mercy on my son...He has seizures and is suffering greatly...I brought him to your disciples, but they could not heal him"* (Matthew 17:15-16).

Jesus rebuked the demon and it came out of the boy immediately.

Then the disciples came to Jesus in private and asked, *"Why couldn't we drive it out?"* (v.19).

He replied, *"Because you have so little faith. I tell you the truth, if you have faith as small as a mustard seed, you can say to this mountain, 'Move from here to there' and it will move. Nothing will be impossible for you"* (v.20).

FROM GOD, TO JESUS, TO YOU

God transferred authority to the name of Jesus, who declared, *"All power is given unto me in heaven and in earth"* (Matthew 28:18 KJV). And, *"If ye shall ask any thing in my name, I will do it"* (John 14:14 KJV).

In turn, He gives the same authority to you and me. Before Jesus ascended to heaven, He said, *"And these signs will accompany those who believe: In my name they will drive out demons; they will speak in new tongues; they will pick up snakes with their hands; and when they drink deadly poison, it will not hurt them at all; they will place their hands on sick people, and they will get well"* (Mark 16:17-18).

These great works are in response to our faith.

CONFIRMING THE WORD

The Lord doesn't allow us the ability to operate in the

miraculous just to demonstrate or show off His power. There is a *purpose* in the will of God.

**When you see the Lord at work,
it not only affects one situation, but
touches countless lives.**

Remember, just before Jesus spoke of the "signs" which would follow those who believe, He said, *"Go into all the world and preach the good news to all creation"* (v.15).

Signs and wonders are how the Lord *confirms* His Word. It is a message to unbelievers that God is still alive, ready to transform their lives.

"GET BEHIND ME!"

As a born again Christian, there's not a reason in the world you should allow Satan and his demons from hell to pressure, coerce, or terrorize you.

Certainly, we need to be aware of his schemes so he will not outwit us (2 Corinthians 2:11). We must recognize the devil for who he is—*"...a murderer from the beginning, not holding to the truth, for there is no truth in him. When he lies, he speaks his native language, for he is a liar and the father of lies"* (John 8:44).

The next time he approaches, take the authority of the Word and say, *"Get behind me, Satan"* (Mark 8:33).

As a believer, the devil has no hold on you. Remember, *"The reason the Son of God appeared was to destroy the devil's work"* (1 John 3:8).

Instead of wasting your time worrying about the tactics of Satan, start praising and worshiping the One who has all power and authority on earth—and in the world to come.

He is the Living God who makes all things possible.

CHAPTER 8

THE POWER OF YOUR TONGUE

T he words flowing out of your mouth are far more than mere conversation. They are a powerful force which can literally change the course of your life—and affect everything around you.

King Solomon wrote, *"The tongue has the power of life and death, and those who love it will eat its fruit"* (Proverbs 18:21).

The Lord will not honor negative comments, but Satan certainly will! In fact, he gleefully welcomes every harsh, bitter, caustic word you utter. Why? Because he wants to destroy your testimony and stain your character.

Over and over, the Bible teaches that what we say—and what we pray—is exactly what we receive. For example, the Lord said, *"...whatever you ask for in prayer, believe that you have received it, and it will be yours"* (Mark 11:24).

If this is true, then people's lives are the way they are

because of what they have spoken, for better or for worse.

We can bless or curse ourselves by what comes out of our mouth because of the power it produces. Since we "eat its fruit," many people are dining on gravel!

YOUR SOURCE OF WISDOM

After years of ministry, I truly believe if men and women really understood that what they say is what they are going to receive they would quickly change their vocabulary.

How about you? Have you been making thoughtless pronouncements without comprehending the consequences?

The Bible asks, *"Who is wise and understanding among you?"* (James 3:13).

There is wisdom which originates in heaven and that which comes from the devil.

THE BOOMERANG!

I can see how a person consumed with hatred and bitterness may seek to curse somebody else, not understanding fully that when they do, their actions bounce back on them. As a result, their life becomes worse than it was before they spoke.

When you speak a judgment, the very thing you say has a boomerang effect—it will fly back to assault you. As Jesus teaches, *"Do not judge, or you too will be judged. For in the same way you judge others, you will be judged, and with the measure you use, it will be measured to you"* (Matthew 7:1-2).

The Lord says, "Speak abundance, not lack." Let me remind you God *"...calls things that are not as though they were"* (Romans 4:17).

THE WRONG INFLUENCE

According to Scripture, people will know what resides in your heart by the words you say. Jesus says, *"...out of the abundance* [what you are thinking and believing] *of the heart the mouth speaketh"* (Matthew 12:34).

You do not necessarily need spiritual discernment to recognize a demonic working; simply watch how a person talks and behaves.

You can detect an influence which is not right—a spirit which needs to be removed because it does not speak as God intends.

James tells you, *"...if you harbor bitter envy and selfish ambition in your hearts, do not boast about it or deny the truth. Such 'wisdom' does not come down from heaven but is earthly..."* (James 3:14-15).

This means the flesh (self) of the prideful person and the words they use are unspiritual and of the devil. *"For where you have envy and selfish ambition, there you find disorder and every evil practice"* (v.16).

PROUD OR HUMBLE?

As we listen to those around us it gives an indication of what is going on inside. When they are envious, they speak jealousy, which means they think somebody else has more than they do.

So instead of trusting the Lord, they try to make things happen themselves. Such individuals need to remember, *"God opposes the proud but gives grace to the humble"* (James 4:6).

It takes humility and submission to admit you need help. And the next step is to ask yourself, "Do I want to continue down this path, or ask God to help me?"

Remember this: *"If we confess our sins, he is faithful and just and will forgive us our sins and purify us from all unrighteousness"* (1 John 1:9).

WHAT ARE YOU SAYING?

You cannot say you are believing God and confess your insufficiency at the same time. When you speak of what you don't possess, you are exercising a form of faith— but not faith in God.

You bind yourself with your own words and make yourself a prisoner to your own curse.

The Almighty has told us that if we have faith in Him (the God-kind of faith), and do not doubt in our heart, mountains will move.

Some people try to put up a good front, yet their damaging words betray them. They need to ask God's forgiveness for the negative thoughts they have spoken, and break the condemnation from their lives.

God will be faithful to pardon them, lifting the scourge and setting them free.

Are you speaking life or death? Are you declaring blessing or cursing? Never forget, the Lord sets those choices before you.

The favor of God comes by faith and is manifest by His love. His power and purpose never inflicts harm, but works for good to destroy the deeds of the devil.

COME BACK TO THE FOLD

Having selfish ambition and envy causes you to think and say you do not have enough. Yet, in Christ we have everything.

When you declare insufficiency, you are denying all Jesus did on the cross, saying He is an unworthy Shepherd who does not take care of you.

Jesus says, *"My sheep listen to my voice; I know them, and they follow me"* (John 10:27).

Could it possibly be your problem is because you are no longer one of His sheep?

Humble yourself, ask His forgiveness, and come back

into the fold. He is saying, *"Return to me....and I will return to you"* (Zechariah 1:3). The Good Shepherd will save, heal and deliver you.

NO MORE GAMES

Whatever promotes self is not God's purpose, plan or part of His Kingdom or glory.

The person who is operating in this kind of wisdom is not going to experience any power from on high. He will wallow in his troubles because he is too prideful or ignorant to acknowledge that he has them.

If you really want to change, then you will examine your inner self, rather than making excuses and blaming others.

You can't play games with God because the contest is over before it begins.

The Lord refuses to assist the person who tries to run his own life because He is not about to share His glory with *anyone.* Let me remind you we are to use the name of Jesus when we pray. Why? Because He tells us, *"...I will do whatever you ask in my name, so that the Son may bring glory to the Father"* (John 14:13).

Excellence in our lives comes to pass according to the purpose and plan of God. To me, that's exciting!

THE SOURCE OF QUARRELS

It can be embarrassing to be in the presence of two people who lose their tempers and become confrontational in public—not seeming to care who overhears their outburst.

Scripture asks, *"What causes fights and quarrels among you?"* (James 4:1).

It happens because hidden within a person is envy, jealousy, or selfish ambition. As the Bible states, *"Pride only breeds quarrels..."* (Proverbs 13:10).

If you desire something you cannot have, try trusting and believing God. Instead of cursing your lack, you should be saying, "Thank you, Lord. I have it by faith in Jesus."

What God wants for you, you will have. And what He knows will harm you, you *should* not receive.

ANOINTED WITH GRACE

The thief has a celebration when he sees discord and strife. The apostle tells husbands and wives to live in harmony so their prayers are not hindered (1 Peter 3:7). He counsels, *"Do not repay evil with evil or insult with insult, but with blessing, because to this you were called so that you may inherit a blessing. For, whoever would love life and see good days must keep his tongue from evil and his lips from deceitful speech"* (vv.9-10).

That's good advice for unmarried people too!

May it be said of you, *"You are the most excellent of men and your lips have been anointed with grace, since God has blessed you forever"* (Psalm 45:2).

Ask the Lord to give you wisdom for every word you speak.

CHAPTER 9

THE HONOR KEY

The secret of opening the door to God's excellence is to give Him the reverence which is due His Holy name.

Before my salvation, I had no concept of honor. Why? Because, *"...there is no one who does good, not even one"* (Psalm 14:3). Remember, *"...for all have sinned and fall short of the glory of God"* (Romans 3:23).

It is to the Father's glory that He has saved you and has forgiven your iniquity: *"I, even I, am he who blots out your transgressions, for my own sake, and remembers your sins no more"* (Isaiah 43:25).

Yes, it is for our redemption, but it is also that He may be exalted. The Almighty says, *"...for my own sake, I do this...I will not yield my glory to another"* (Isaiah 48:11). God loves us, yet He must receive all the honor and praise.

This is why we proclaim, *"Glory to God in the highest"* (Luke 2:14) and shout, *"Hosanna to the Son of David! Blessed is he who comes in the name of the Lord! Hosanna in the highest!"* (Matthew 21:9).

Before God's power can cause blessing, honor must be offered.

Let me share five specific ways you can demonstrate your love and respect for the Lord:

1. Honor God with your thoughts.

What occupies your mind on an average day? Are you consumed with coordinating your children's hectic schedules—or the phone calls you have to return?

In our "busyness" it is easy to forget the One who gave us life. That's why we need to take a deep breath, slow down and give honor to our Maker. We are told, *"Thou wilt keep him in perfect peace, whose mind is stayed on thee: because he trusteth in thee"* (Isaiah 26:3 KJV).

Instead of allowing your mind to be pulled down to the carnality of this world, Paul tells you to dwell on what is "excellent." He says, *"...whatever is true, whatever is noble, whatever is right, whatever is pure, whatever is lovely, whatever is admirable—if anything is excellent or praiseworthy—think about such things"* (Philippians 4:8).

Today, *"...fix your thoughts on Jesus"* (Hebrews 3:1) and spend some quality time thinking of what He means in your life—His love, His grace, and His provision.

2. Honor the Lord with your body.

God's Word warns of the danger of using our bodies

for what is dishonorable—lying, cheating, violence or sexual perversion. These do not bring esteem to the Lord.

Paul writes, *"Do you not know that your body is a temple of the Holy Spirit, who is in you, whom you have received from God? You are not your own; you were bought at a price. Therefore honor God with your body"* (1 Corinthians 6:19-20).

We are to use this "temple of clay" for what is proper and beneficial.

The Bible tells us, *"... God anointed Jesus of Nazareth with the Holy Spirit and power, and how he went around doing good"* (Acts 10:38). If our spirit, mind and body belong to the Lord, this is also how we are to behave.

You were created to be *"...to the praise of his glory"* (Ephesians 1:12), and a *"vessel unto honour, sanctified, and meet for the master's use, and prepared unto every good work"* (2 Timothy 2:21 KJV).

You must not forget, as a believer, God lives in you and you are to be His representative on earth.

3. Honor God with your finances.

When the law of life begins to flow in your body, you will walk in divine forgiveness, health and in financial supply.

As you honor God with the first fruits of your substance (the tithe that belongs to the Lord), you will also receive. Jesus says, *"Give, and it will be given to you. A good measure, pressed down, shaken together and running over, will be poured into your lap. For with the measure you use, it will be measured to you"* (Luke 6:38).

I recognize God's financial provision in my life and acknowledge Him as my provider. My work is not my supplier, but my Lord certainly is. Even so, my Father furnishes me with income so I can honor Him.

It is God who bestows on us the ability to acquire wealth (Deuteronomy 8). As such, we are to be channels of His abundance on earth—in the physical realm.

Our giving is a form of the excellence He expects. As Paul writes: *"But just as you excel in everything—in faith, in speech, in knowledge, in complete earnestness and in your love for us—see that you also excel in this grace of giving"* (2 Corinthians 8:7).

4. Honor God in your relationships.

The only occasion the disciples ever asked for more faith was when Jesus taught concerning forgiveness (Luke 16:3-5)—not when He cast out devils, raised the dead, healed the sick or calmed the storms.

Why was this true? Because we need special power when we are dealing with people. The Lord says,

"...whatever you did for one of the least of these...you did for me" (Matthew 25:40).

We are to humble ourselves under the hand of the Almighty and prefer others. *"Be devoted to one another in brotherly love. Honor one another above yourselves"* (Romans12:10).

This is demonstrated as we forgive someone for words spoken against us or injustices done towards us.

Forgiveness takes supernatural power because we do not have it in ourselves apart from what the Father gives.

Reverence goes to God when we acknowledge Him in *all* our ways.

5. Honor God through worship and praise.

We demonstrate our love and admiration for the Lord when we say with the psalmist, *"Let God be exalted!"* (Psalmist 70:4).

Every time we lift our hearts and voices to heaven we: *"Ascribe to the Lord the glory due his name;* [and] *worship the Lord in the splendor of his holiness"* (Psalm 29:2).

In addition to the expression of our soul, we honor the Lord with the sacrifice of ourselves. As Paul explains, *"Therefore, I urge you, brothers, in view of God's mercy, to offer your bodies as living sacrifices, holy and pleasing to God—this is your spiritual act of worship"* (Romans 12:1).

One day, we will see the Lord face to face, and be able to sing with the angel chorus, *"Worthy is the Lamb, who was slain, to receive power and wealth and wisdom and strength and honor and glory and praise!"* (Revelation 5:12).

What a glorious day that will be!

THE BATTLE

Don't be deceived. There is a demonic power stalking the earth whose only aim is to sow seeds of discord and dishonor—toward God and our fellow man.

When people think about evil or say "deliver us from our enemies," they are referring to individuals. Paul tells us, *"For we wrestle not against flesh and blood* [people], *but against principalities, against powers, against the rulers of the darkness of this world, against spiritual wickedness in high places"* (Ephesians 6:12 KJV).

Satan uses people for his selfish purposes because he does not care for their well being.

His objective is to steal, kill and destroy (John 10:10) and separate us from God.

What a sharp contrast from the Father who cares for

us with an everlasting love.

AN EYE FOR AN EYE?

When Jesus was teaching on the subject of prayer, He said, *"Forgive us our sins, for we also forgive everyone who sins against us"* (Luke 11:4). Then He added, *"And lead us not into temptation"* (v.4).

A definition of temptation is "dealing with evil." This is why the Word states God does not tempt any man with evil (James 1:13). To the contrary, He gives us authority over Satan.

Jesus tells us specifically how to deal with evil. In His Sermon on the Mount, He declared, *"You have heard that it was said, 'Eye for eye, and tooth for tooth.' But I tell you, Do not resist an evil person. If someone strikes you on the right cheek, turn to him the other also. And if someone wants to sue you and take your tunic, let him have your cloak as well. If someone forces you to go one mile, go with him two miles. Give to the one who asks you, and do not turn away from the one who wants to borrow from you"* (Matthew 5:38-42).

Then He added these profound words: *"You have heard that it was said, 'Love your neighbor and hate your enemy.' But I tell you: Love your enemies and pray for those who persecute you, that you may be sons of your Father in heaven"* (vv.43-45).

THE BEST PART!

I am convinced that before you can have power in relationships with people, you need to receive the forgiveness of God through Christ—and demonstrate this gift by honoring the Father and forgiving others.

Here's the best part! When you revere the Lord, He will return the favor. *"He will call upon me, and I will answer him; I will be with him in trouble, I will deliver him and honor him"* (Psalm 91:15).

It is the key to God's eternal blessing.

CHAPTER 10

QUALITY THOUGHTS, WORDS AND DEEDS

Once, when Jesus and His disciples were walking from Judea to Galilee, they passed through a town in Samaria called Sychar.

The Lord was tired, and sat down to rest by Jacob's well, while the disciples went into the village to buy some food. When they were gone He asked for a drink of water from a woman who had come to draw from the well. She was stunned, since Jews did not associate with Samaritans.

However, Jesus told her, *"Everyone who drinks this water will be thirsty again, but whoever drinks the water I give him will never thirst. Indeed, the water I give him will become in him a spring of water welling up to eternal life"* (John 4:13-14).

As Jesus continued to talk about spiritual matters, the

woman said, *"I know that Messiah (called Christ) is coming. When he comes, he will explain everything to us"* (v.25).

Then Jesus declared, *"I who speak to you am he"* (v.26).

NOURISHMENT FROM ABOVE

Immediately, the Samaritan woman ran back to the city to tell the people what she had just heard. Soon the disciples returned with the food they had purchased and when they urged Jesus to eat something, He said to them, *"I have food to eat that you know nothing about"* (v.32).

Surprised, the disciples looked at each other and asked, "Could someone have brought Him a meal?"

The Lord answered with these powerful, insightful words: *"My food...is to do the will of him who sent me and to finish his work"* (v.34).

You see, Jesus gained strength and nourishment from doing the will of God—seeing the Kingdom of heaven advanced by bringing light to the lost. In the process, He did not do or say anything which was not in the ultimate plan of His Father. He was living the words of the psalmist: *"I desire to do your will, O my God"* (Psalm 40:8).

BLESSING UPON BLESSING

When you have God's purpose at heart—as Jesus did—the Almighty gives you the grace and ability to be blessed spiritually, mentally, emotionally, physically, financially and in relationships.

God orders your steps and directs your path. If you obey His commands, constant favor will be yours: *"You will be blessed in the city and blessed in the country...You will be blessed when you come in and blessed when you go out"* (Deuteronomy 28:3,6).

This is the result of a life which is purposed for the Almighty.

When you know you are here for a reason, the fire of God consumes you and the love of the Father constrains and compels you.

You are on a mission from heaven to spread His message by thoughts, words, and deeds. You are here to magnify and glorify the Lord who has loved and redeemed you.

As a result of "joyful obedience," you become the person whom the Lord does miracles for and through. *"God is able to make all grace abound to you, so that in all things at all times, having all that you need, you will abound in every good work"* (2 Corinthians 9:8).

This does not mean you occasionally do something for the Lord when you feel in the mood, but *constantly!* Everywhere you journey, your life is to be a blessing— touching others for the Savior.

SEED TO THE SOWER

As it is written: *"He has scattered abroad his gifts to the poor; his righteousness endures forever"* (v.9). Even more, He equips you for this good work: *"Now he who supplies seed to the sower* [the supplier is God, and the sower is you] *and bread for food will also supply and increase your store of seed and will enlarge the harvest of your righteousness. You will be made rich in every way so that you can be generous on every occasion, and through us your generosity will result in thanksgiving to God"* (vv.10-11).

People will praise the Lord for what He has miraculously accomplished through you.

ALL THINGS BEAUTIFUL

Have you ever felt as if you were living in "limbo"—drifting somewhere between where you once were and where you are supposed to be?

During such an unsettling period, when you are not rooted or grounded and everything seems to be coming unglued, it can be either an experience of blessing or cursing, depending on what you allow to happen.

This is the moment to stand firmly on the promises of God who goes ahead of us, preparing the way. We do not need to be afraid, discouraged, or think we are by ourselves. The Lord has a blueprint and purpose—and He makes all things beautiful in its season.

"FIXED" THOUGHTS

Stay anchored in the Word and do not become distracted or defeated. Praise, worship and thank Him, as you go about your daily activities. Don't cave in and permit yourself to become engulfed with negative thoughts—such as worrying unnecessarily over your health, your finances and your family.

Life, and its myriad distractions can cause us to lose focus if we do not *"...fix our eyes on Jesus, the author and perfecter of our faith"* (Hebrews 12:2). *"Thou wilt keep him in perfect peace, whose mind is stayed* [or fixed] *on thee"* (Isaiah 26:3 KJV).

Center your thoughts on the covenants and promises of God. Be excited about what He has in store for you, and allow Him to take you through every valley.

Listen, as the Lord reassures, *"Be strong and courageous. Do not be afraid or discouraged..."* (2 Chronicles 32:7). *"...I am with you; do not be dismayed, for I am your God. I will strengthen you and help you; I will uphold you with my righteous right hand"* (Isaiah 41:10).

The Father is not only in your present, but has already lived in your *future.* Since He knows where the road is leading, *"Trust in the Lord with all your heart and lean not on your own understanding; in all your ways acknowledge him, and he will make your paths straight"* (Proverbs 3:5-6).

With this blessed assurance, we can be confident tomorrow is going to be better than today!

QUALITY FRUIT!

If you are living according to the will of God, people will know you because of the spiritual manifestation of your life. Jesus said, *"By their fruit you will recognize them"* (Matthew 7:16).

God places His quality inside each of His children by allowing them to possess the fruit of the Spirit. They will enjoy, *"...love, joy, peace, patience, kindness, goodness, faithfulness, gentleness and self-control"* (Galatians 5:23).

Peter asks us to *"...add to your faith goodness; and to goodness, knowledge; and to knowledge, self-control; and to self-control, perseverance; and to perseverance, godliness; and to godliness, brotherly kindness; and to brotherly kindness, love. For if you possess these qualities in increasing measure, they will keep you from being ineffective and unproductive in your knowledge of our Lord Jesus Christ"* (2 Peter 1:5-8).

When we try to produce these attributes within ourselves, we fail miserably. It is the Son of God residing in our inner-man which allows the seeds of the fruit of the Spirit to grow. This nurturing begins the moment we are born again. As Paul declared, *"I have been crucified with Christ and I no longer live, but Christ lives in me. The life I live in the body, I live by faith in the Son of God, who loved me and gave himself for me"* (Galatians 2:20).

It is the Lord who places His best in you. Never forget, *"God's kindness leads you toward repentance"* (Romans 2:4).

Today I am earnestly praying that your thoughts, words and deeds will reflect the marvelous transformation the Lord has made in you.

CHAPTER 11

DEVELOPING HIS EXCELLENCE IN YOU

T he longer you study Scripture, the more you realize that men and women in Bible times were known and remembered for certain qualities and actions—whether good or bad. For example:

- Cain was known for his anger and jealousy. Because of this weakness, he murdered his brother Abel.
- Abraham was noted for his unshakable faith, and the Lord called him His friend.
- Esther was a beautiful woman of God inside and out. She had a quiet and obedient spirit and exhibited no fear.
- David was known as a worshiper, of whom God said, "He has My heart."

- Joshua was heralded for his courage—marching into the Promised Land and returning it to God's people.
- Timothy was remembered for his genuine care for fellow believers.
- Peter—even with his faults—had a bold confession.

TRUST AND OBEDIENCE

Inside every person, there are certain characteristics and traits which set them apart. And you can identify those whose hearts are turned toward the Lord.

Daniel was such a man—totally trustworthy. The Bible records he, *"...so distinguished himself among the administrators and the satraps by his exceptional qualities that the king planned to set him over the whole kingdom"* (Daniel 6:3).

In fact, he became the chief advisor to *three* kings and outlived them all. Daniel had precisely the qualities needed; and his position was strengthened by the wisdom of God.

Consider Jacob. Even after making the mistake of trying to steal his brother's inheritance, he finally learned to receive blessings God's way. When Jacob realized how he was supposed to live, the Father's favor rested upon him. Jacob learned obedience rather than leaning on his own understanding.

A FORGIVING SPIRIT

Think of the qualities of Joseph—an incredible man of God. He went through the pits of hell, yet the Lord finally exalted him until he was in charge of the government of Egypt, saving his people from starvation.

Even after being betrayed by his brothers, the Lord had placed such a forgiving spirit within him, he was able to look at his brothers and say, *"You intended to harm me, but God intended it for good to accomplish what is now being done, the saving of many lives"* (Genesis 50:20). And the next verse is also important: *"'So then, don't be afraid. I will provide for you and your children.' And he reassured them and spoke kindly to them"* (v.51).

A faithful heart forgives and does not allow bitterness, resentment and anger to take root and become master.

WHAT ABOUT YOU?

These real individuals are examples for us so we may learn about faith, hope, and the love of God (1 Corinthians 10:6,11).

Since I was young, I was taught, "Even a child is known by his ways."

What quality do people see when they encounter you? If they spotted you in a grocery story, would their hearts be lifted, or would they quickly run down a different aisle?

Your witness for Christ is intrinsically linked to your character.

Every event in your life happens for a reason. God can even take what is negative and replace it with His qualities.

Paul is a prime example. As Saul, he was a troublemaker, persecuting those who followed Christ. Yet, after the Damascus Road experience, Paul became a miracle-worker, demonstrating the Spirit of God in power. With perseverance, He took the Gospel to the nations of the world.

At times, the Lord will make things known to us we would rather He didn't. However, He only shows us what needs to be changed or refined—and His grace will enable the transformation to occur.

A PERMANENT RECORD

If you give the Lord a chance, He will work out His quality in you as a testimony to His glory—and it will be displayed in Jesus' name.

Unless the Lord returns before your life ends, there will be something written on your epitaph, whether carved in stone or etched on someone's heart.

People will remember you for who you were and the principles on which you stood. What quality of the

Father are they going to recall in you?

Do you want to be known as a godly man or woman, honest and reliable? A person of peace? Joy? Integrity?

A SPECIAL CREATION

You might think you are not worthy, but the God you serve is—and He has distinguished you. In the words of the psalmist, *"Know that the Lord has set apart the godly for himself"* (Psalm 4:3).

The individuals we have mentioned from Scripture have unique qualities, and so do you. The Lord has created each of us in a very special way to accomplish His purpose. It is through us He displays Himself to the world. If we are living according to His will, every person we meet has a glimpse of the Lord.

Before Christ (B.C.) we were nothing but poor, miserable, wretched sinners, which means we did not care about God or have anything to do with Him.

Since we were not in the Father's image, Jesus said, "You must be born again." It is not an option.

Oh, you may try to act superior, saying, "Look who I am. See what I have accomplished," yet in the Lord's sight it is meaningless and insignificant. God looks on, shaking His head.

RIGHTFUL HEIRS

Imagine Almighty God, who created the universe just by speaking the Word, is mindful of you and me! How awesome it is that the Almighty would distinguish us in this way—not because of who we are, how much money we possess, how virtuous we may be or how much fame, abilities or education we have accrued. It is not about our accomplishments, rather for His name's sake and His glory we were created.

We are distinguished in that He has loved us through Jesus (God in the flesh) who died for us on the cross, rose from the dead and is seated in all glory and honor in His rightful place as King of kings and Lord of lords. He says, "These are My children whom I have set my everlasting love upon, whom I have given Myself for, that he or she might have My life."

Even more, the good work God has begun in us He is faithful to perfect and complete (Philippians 1:6).

How marvelous to know we are created by God's workmanship—spirit, mind and body.

What a privilege to be His son or daughter through the blood of Christ. *"But as many as received him* [Jesus], *to them gave he power to become the sons of God, even to them that believe on his name"* (John 1:12 KJV).

Because of this we have all the rights and benefits of heaven. We are His legal heirs and the Father has not withheld anything from His children.

AN AMAZING TRANSFORMATION

The Lord is ready to pour His character into you when you submit yourself to Him and say, "Thank You, Lord, for forgiving, loving and offering me a new beginning and all it holds in Your divine plan and purpose. Thank you, Lord, You are developing Your character within me."

Praise God, He never forsakes or abandons us. He is believing all things, hoping all things, bearing all things; He is going to see good come to pass because that is who He is. When His character is working in you, there will be a glorious change:

- Where there was fear there is faith (Isaiah 54:14).
- Where there was guilt there is grace (Hebrews 8:12).
- Where there was conflict there is comfort (Psalm 37:24).
- Where there was death there is deliverance (Psalm 49:15).
- Where there was trouble there is triumph (Psalm 37:39).
- Where there was loneliness there is love (1 John 4:10).
- Where there was sin there is salvation (2 Corinthians 5:21).

It is important to make certain the quality and character of God resides within you because one day you will stand before the Lord and give an account of the time you have spent on earth. The Bible says your life *"...will be shown for what it is, because the Day will bring it to light. It will be revealed with fire, and the fire will test the quality of each man's work"* (1 Corinthians 3:13).

Will you pass the exam which determines how you will spend eternity?

CHAPTER 12

NO MORE FEAR!

In the days of Isaac, a great famine spread across the land. It was so devastating that he went to Abimelech, king of the Philistines in Gerar and told him he was moving his family to Egypt.

But God appeared to Isaac, telling him, *"Do not go down to Egypt; live in the land where I tell you to live. Stay in this land for a while, and I will be with you and will bless you. For to you and your descendants I will give all these lands and will confirm the oath I swore to your father Abraham. I will make your descendants as numerous as the stars in the sky and will give them all these lands, and through your offspring all nations on earth will be blessed, because Abraham obeyed me and kept my requirements, my commands, my decrees and my laws"* (Genesis 26:2-5).

So Isaac remained in Gerar, where he planted crops in the arid, parched ground, and, by a miracle, reaped a huge harvest. In fact, Isaac became rich and grew increasingly prosperous until he accumulated large flocks, herds and many servants.

As you can imagine, the Philistines began to envy this wealthy man—so much so they reaped revenge by throwing dirt and debris into all the wells on his land which had been dug back in the days of his father, Abraham (v.15).

At this point, King Abimelech, ordered Isaac, *"Move away from us; you have become too powerful for us"* (v.16).

In truth, it was God Almighty who had made Isaac so wealthy in the sight of the king.

Abimelech was not able to readily accept what happened to Isaac. It would have been far better if he had admitted, "If God blesses somebody one-hundred-fold in a time of famine, I want to know how it happened. I want to be blessed too."

However, many are frightened of what they do not understand. In Acts 5, people were afraid to enter the church because of the fear of God and the miracles which were taking place.

A PLACE OF PEACE

Back on the plains of Palestine, this was a time of great worry for Isaac and his family as they left familiar territory to start over in a forsaken valley. Then one day, as his servants were digging, they came upon a well of spring water. The shepherds of Gerar argued with Isaac's shepherds, shouting "This water is ours!" When they uncovered the next well, the same disagreement arose.

Where there is quarreling, there is fear, not faith.

Finally, Isaac dug a third well and called it Rehoboth—because no one argued over it. The name meant: *"Now the Lord has given us room and we will flourish in the land"* (v.22).

This was the place where God wanted him to be: a safe haven, the land of peace, where he could grow and prosper once more.

FROM GENERATION TO GENERATION

From there Isaac went up to Beersheba where the Lord appeared to him again and said, *"I am the God of your father Abraham. Do not be afraid, for I am with you; I will bless you and will increase the number of your descendants for the sake of my servant Abraham"* (v.24).

In other words, "Relax. I made this promise to your father—and the same pledge is also for you."

From generation to generation, descendants will be blessed because of the obedience of God's people and the faithfulness of the Father who lavishes His love upon us.

Isaac built an altar and called on the name of the Lord. He pitched his tent in Beersheba and his servants began digging another well.

A RECONCILIATION

Suddenly, King Abimelech appeared. He had traveled from Gerar with his personal advisor and the commander of his forces. Isaac asked them, *"Why have you come to me, since you were hostile to me and sent me away?"* (v.27).

They answered, *"We saw clearly that the Lord was with you; so we said, 'There ought to be a sworn agreement between us...Let us make a treaty with you that you will do us no harm, just as we did not molest you but always treated you well and sent you away in peace. And now you are blessed by the Lord'"* (vv.28-29).

The Bible records Isaac then made a feast for them, and they ate and drank.

God prepared a table before Isaac in the presence of his enemies—in this case, jealous men who thought he had become too prosperous.

Let's face it, if the blessings of the Lord are on your life, it makes some people uncomfortable. It may take a while for them to recognize what God is truly doing.

This is an example for you and me. If you have unresolved issues in your life, take the initiative to make things right. Confront the matter with a heart of peace, not with antagonism, bitterness, resentment, or selfishness. Otherwise it will only lead to strife.

A GODLY TESTIMONY

When God's love is at work, people's hearts and

minds are changed.

Those unbelieving Philistines observed how Isaac had left in peace. It communicated a great lesson to them. Instead of arguing over "Who is right? Who is wrong?" he departed with a godly testimony.

That same day, Isaac's servants came and told him about digging the well and finding water. When were they successful? After peace was settled.

This is important to God. As His Word declares: *"When a man's ways are pleasing to the Lord, he makes even his enemies live at peace with him"* (Proverbs 16:7).

FAREWELL TO FEAR

The Lord's secret weapon against worry and anxiety is true love. We are told: *"There is no fear in love; but perfect love casteth out fear: because fear hath torment"* (1 John 4:18 KJV).

The lives of millions are in anguish because they do not know what the future holds. But every time they express their fear, it's a sure sign they are not receiving the love God offers—because His love eliminates *all* fear.

Each time you worry, you are denying the love of your Father in heaven. You are saying, "Lord, you can't take care of me—I will have to do it myself."

When this happens, you start bickering and fighting —and lose the blessing. Just as serious of a matter, anxiety can affect your health because negative emotions allow the thief entrance to steal, kill and destroy.

By reaching out to the Lord in faith and receiving the love He has for you through trust and obedience, all fear evaporates.

A BUMPER CROP

During the time of famine, when Isaac looked at his dire situation, he had to stretch his faith to sow seed. And the only way he could activate such belief and expectation was to eliminate anxiety.

As long as he doubted and feared, he was not believing the promises of God. He was thinking "pull in" rather than "give out." But when Isaac understood the Lord's perfect love for him—even in a time of great famine—he began to prepare for a bumper crop.

It does not matter what the circumstance or situation happens to be, the Lord is on your side.

And, *"If God is for us, who can be against us?"* (Romans 8:31).

Can poverty, sickness or any demonic host cause us harm? They have no power!

THE BEGINNING OF WISDOM

There are two distinct types of fear mentioned in the Word. One refers to the worry and anxiety over the concerns of life. The other is a healthy fear—the fear of the Almighty.

This means we are to worship, reverence, respect and honor God. Remember, *"The fear of the Lord is the beginning of wisdom; all who follow his precepts have good understanding"* (Psalm 111:10).

Isaac had such total respect for the Father—and it led to favor beyond measure. I pray you will receive God's richest blessings too.

CHAPTER 13

WHAT IS YOUR RESPONSE?

In my early years of ministry I must admit I operated with perhaps more zeal than wisdom. After reading how Jesus was anointed of the Spirit to do good, destroy the works of the devil and heal all who were oppressed (Acts 10:38), I wanted to operate in the same manner.

I said to the Lord, "Your Spirit is upon me and we are going to set the captives free!" (Luke 4:18).

Since this was rooted and grounded in my heart, and I felt I was there to do the will of the Lord, I was ready to appropriate and apply what had been given to Jesus.

I was convinced it was time to take any person who was having problems and see them saved, healed and delivered. I was going to attack the devil and send him packing from people's lives. I was ready to see families restored, relationships blessed, finances ship-shape and running over with blessing—so they could help spread the Gospel to the nations and give to the needy.

This is how I first approached people, but I ran into trouble!

I quickly found out that not everybody wants to be helped or desires to have financial blessings, and healthy, wonderful relationships with peace and joy in their minds and hearts.

I was surprised to learn that many would rather grumble, complain and wallow in self-pity—acting in their selfish interests rather than what God wants.

One man told me, "Don't be so pushy!"

There I was, trying to see him saved, but he didn't believe he needed spiritual help. Others felt their lives were in order when God was saying just the opposite.

I could not understand the resistance since all I was trying to do was to see their lives controlled by the Holy Spirit instead of Satan.

A MATTER OF CHOICE

During this process, the Lord taught me a valuable lesson. He said, "Son, your desire is wonderful, and the zeal in your life for Me is fantastic. Your heart and love for Me is admirable. You are responding to what I have given, but when you share with others you have to understand I have given them a free choice. You cannot force their acceptance."

The Lord finally taught me how He operates, and now I do the same. I present the things of God which are real, available and have the power to change lives. The next step is up to them.

I can't make a person become a Christian—it is a matter of choice:

- *"This day I call heaven and earth as witnesses against you that I have set before you life and death, blessings and curses. Now choose life, so that you and your children may live"* (Deuteronomy 30:19).
- *"...choose for yourselves this day whom you will serve...But as for me and my household, we will serve the Lord"* (Joshua 24:15).
- *"For whosoever shall call upon the name of the Lord shall be saved"* (Romans 10:13 KJV).

The decision is yours.

THE FIRST STEP

Today, I respect a person's right to go to hell—or to heaven. God has given them the option. It's not my place to knock someone over the head, tie him up and carry him across the finish line to be with the Lord forever more!

Oh, there are times I'd like to apply a little pressure when I see someone who is stubborn, rebellious and self-willed—and they don't realize how damned they really are. But I am not the judge.

Jesus came, lived, did the work and will of God, and showed people who the Father is. He never coerced, compelled or interfered with anyone's life.

Christ died to save us, rose from the dead, and ascended back to His seat at the right hand of the Father. God simply says, *"Whoever is thirsty, let him come; and whoever wishes, let him take the free gift of the water of life"* (Revelation 22:17).

You can lead a sinner to the precious fountain, but you can't make him drink!

Even though you have presented the answer, it's up to the hurting person to ask for help. God Himself is not going to invade his life.

I refuse to counsel those who do not want guidance and advice. They must make the initial step.

"IT'S YOUR MOVE!"

In the midst of terrible circumstances, I've heard people say, "Where is God? Why doesn't He do something?"

Again, the person with a need must reach out to the

Lord. Scripture says, *"Come near to God and he will come near to you"* (James 4:8).

It's your move! *"...to all who received him, to those who believed in his name, he gave the right to become children of God"* (John 1:12).

He offers the provision, which must be accepted by faith. Why? Because *"...without faith it is impossible to please God, because anyone who comes to him must believe that he exists and that he rewards those who earnestly seek him"* (Hebrews 11:6).

You have to desire Him—*earnestly!*

"CALL ON ME"

The same process is involved regarding spiritual gifts. If you want these present and active in your life, you must *"eagerly desire"* them (1 Corinthians 14:1).

The Lord will give you power, yet you must take the initiative: *"...they that wait upon the Lord shall renew their strength; they shall mount up with wings as eagles; they shall run, and not be weary; and they shall walk, and not faint"* (Isaiah 40:31 KJV).

This pattern of God requiring personal action is prevalent throughout Scripture. The Lord says, *"...call upon me and come and pray to me, and I will listen to you. You will seek me and find me when you seek me with all your heart"* (Jeremiah 29:12-13). And He declares, *"Call to me and I will answer you and tell you great and unsearchable things you do not know"* (Jeremiah 33:3).

HIS MIGHTY NAME

Jesus was sent to earth by His father, yet He does not force Himself on you. Instead, He says, *"Come to me, all you who are weary and burdened, and I will give you rest"* (Matthew 11:28).

How do you approach Him? Simply speak the name of Jesus. All authority and access in heaven and earth has been given through His name to those who believe in Him. The name and the Person are the same.

Just before Jesus ascended back to heaven, He told the believers, *"In that day you will no longer ask me anything. I tell you the truth, my Father will give you whatever you ask in my name"* (John 16:23).

You don't have to go through any earthly priest or substitute.

Today, you can receive the qualities of God through the resurrection power of Jesus' name.

"HERE I AM"

I love the portion of Psalm 91 where the Lord is speaking: *"Because he loves me...I will rescue him; I will protect him, for he acknowledges my name. He will call upon me, and I will answer him; I will be with him in trouble, I will deliver him and honor him. With long life will I satisfy him and show him my salvation"* (Psalm 91:14-16).

The Lord has done everything necessary. Now He is

searching to and fro, back and forth across the earth for someone in whom—and through whom—He can show Himself mighty (2 Chronicles 16:9).

God is looking for the one He can bless, who cries out, "Here I am. Thank you, Lord."

We must realize His work has already been accomplished. It is not that God is *going* to heal your body or save your soul. He has *already* redeemed and delivered you. All you need to do is accept what He has finished. It is a gift He has prepared. As I like to say, "It's all wrapped up with a Holy Ghost bow on it."

The present is yours through Jesus. Just believe, receive, accept it and say:

- I receive my healing.
- I receive my salvation.
- I receive freedom from oppression and depression.
- I receive my life.
- I receive my friends and relationships.
- I receive peace and love.

Every once in a while, I meet a person who complains, "I received what the Lord offered, but it didn't work."

They may have accepted the package, but did they

open it up? I've seen beautiful leather Bibles in homes I have visited, yet what is the value if they just sit on a shelf collecting dust and are never read?

The Word must be allowed to enter your heart. That means you must study it's treasures and allow them to permeate your life.

The marvelous work of God has already been completed. Now the Lord is waiting for your response.

What will it be?

CHAPTER 14

DOING WHAT'S RIGHT!

W e live in a generation where issues are clouded, yet we need to see a distinction between the righteous and the wicked, a demarcation between those who are believers and those who are not.

Many who profess to be Christians are allowing their lives to be infiltrated with what God considers an abomination. They quietly conform to the world and in some cases actually agree with their carnality. Some say they believe the Word of God, yet only accept certain parts of Scripture—then do whatever they desire.

How can they expect to receive the blessing of God?

"OFF THE FENCE"

We cannot just pick and choose the commandments and divine principles by which we wish to live. Jesus is either our Lord and Savior, or He is not. If He truly is, our response must be, "I believe His Word, and that

113

settles the matter. Where I have been lukewarm or compromised, I am going to make a change."

It's time to stop straddling the fence. As Moses asked the disobedient children of Israel who had made a golden idol, *"Who is on the Lord's side?"* (Exodus 32:26).

If you claim to be a Christian, put away what is not of Him and start walking according to God's precepts. As Jesus declares, *"If ye continue in my word, then are ye my disciples indeed; And ye shall know the truth, and the truth shall make you free"* (John 8:31-21 KJV).

THIEVES IN THE PEW

Let me be blunt. God's Word specifically tells us the tithe belongs to the Lord, yet research studies show only a small percent of church members actually pay their tithes.

For a number of years, the Barna Research group has been following the practice of tithing (donating at least ten percent of one's income). They recently reported (www.barna.org), "While Christians dispute whether tithing refers to giving the entire ten percent to churches or whether that sum may include money donated to churches and other non-profit entities, the survey data reveal that no matter how it is defined, very few Americans tithed in 2004. Only 4% gave such an amount to churches alone; just 6% gave to either churches or to a combination of churches and parachurch ministries."

To say the Almighty is not pleased is putting it

mildly. He says: *"Will a man rob God? Yet you rob me. But you ask, 'How do we rob you?' In tithes and offerings"* (Malachi 3:8).

As a result, the Lord declares, *"You are under a curse—the whole nation of you—because you are robbing me. Bring the whole tithe into the storehouse, that there may be food in my house"* (vv. 9-10).

Since the Father is the source of every blessing, and all things come from His throne, it only makes sense that we honor Him with His tithes and our offerings.

Just think what God could do if every believer on the face of the earth would obey His command regarding finances.

The work of the church would explode and the impact of the Gospel would multiply incredibly.

STRIKE THREE!

The options are stark indeed. The Lord declares if you tithe, you will be blessed. The devil says if you give, you will be cursed.

Since Satan knows he is already doomed, he attempts to bring as many down with him as possible. But three strikes and he's out:

- Strike one: He was banished from heaven (Isaiah 14:12).
- Strike two: He was defeated at the cross (Colossians 2:15).
- Strike three: When Christ returns the devil will be sentenced to hell (Revelation 20:10).

Those who follow and obey Satan are going to end up with him in the lake of fire, a place of outer darkness and everlasting punishment. That's not where I want to spend eternity!

A STERN WARNING

Some who call themselves Christians fail miserably in the trespasses listed by the apostle Paul. He writes: *"The acts of the sinful nature are obvious: sexual immorality, impurity and debauchery; idolatry and witchcraft; hatred, discord, jealousy, fits of rage, selfish ambition, dissensions, factions and envy; drunkenness, orgies, and the like. I warn you, as I did before, that those who live like this will not inherit the kingdom of God"* (Genesis 5:19-21).

Sadly, there are believers who lie to their associates and cheat on their taxes, yet seem to be oblivious to their behavior.

If you are God's child, the Lord—who does what is right—is supposed to be living in you. How can you expect Him to remain in your heart, mind and soul if you constantly choose to disobey?

WORSHIPING IN VAIN

Many are tottering on the brink of disaster and they don't even know it. They sit in church every week and sing praises, but there is sin in their lives they have not asked God to forgive and remove. The Lord says such people are like those He encountered at the temple, who *"...honor me with their lips, but their hearts are far from me. They worship me in vain; their teachings are but rules taught by men"* (Matthew 15:8-9).

TIME FOR CONFESSION

David cried, *"Do not cast me from your presence or take your Holy Spirit from me"* (Psalm 51:11).

After nine months of self-denial, trying to cover his sin with Bathsheba and having Uriah killed, David finally came to his senses and confessed his sin to God. He writes, *"When I kept silent, my bones wasted away through my groaning all day long. For day and night your hand was heavy upon me; my strength was sapped as in the heat of summer. Then I acknowledged my sin to you and did not cover up my iniquity. I said, 'I will confess my transgressions to the Lord'—and you forgave the guilt of my sin"* (Psalm 32:3-5).

The Father not only pardoned David, but restored him to a place of divine leadership.

MAKING THINGS RIGHT

God forbid we ever get to the point where our conscience is so seared we feel no guilt over doing what is wrong. If that day ever arrives you need to seriously ask yourself, "Am I truly a born-again Christian?"

Think about a time you failed to act on a promise or an order which was required but convinced yourself, "It's okay, I'll just skip it."

It is the Lord who gently whispers, "Come back and do what is right." He will nudge your conscience until you finish the task.

"REPENT BOLDLY!"

Martin Luther once said, "If you are going to sin, sin boldly. Let the whole world know what you did." Then he counseled, "Repent boldly. Let the world know your actions were wrong and you are sorry."

Identify the transgression, then deal with it. Acknowledge if you are paralyzed with fear, filled with lust, or harbor greed, hatred, or bitterness. Otherwise, you will be riddled with guilt.

Some try to avoid dealing with the consequences by saying "There is no God"—continuing down their wicked path. They would even abolish the laws of society if possible. However, they can never run away from themselves, and the sin-consciousness the Creator placed within them. At some point they will have an appointment with God.

Those who refuse to admit their transgressions will face far more than their current problems.

They may stand before the Lord and list their good works, asking, "Didn't we do these things in Your name?" But the Lord will look at them and say, "I don't know who you are. Depart from me, you workers of iniquity!" (Luke 13:27).

SECRET FAULTS

Certain internal issues may be hidden from you—things which have happened in the past which you may not be fully aware of. David looked to heaven and prayed, *"Who can discern his errors? Forgive my hidden faults"* (Psalm19:12).

These failings refer to those that are not on a conscious level.

Have you ever said something and wondered where in the world the words came from? Perhaps it was a concealed hurt down in your heart where the devil planted a seed and it began to grow. You didn't even know it was festering there.

Tragically, many have blotted out childhood sexual abuse, then years later it suddenly becomes a raging manifestation. These are hidden faults only a loving God can remove.

TOTAL PARDON

The Lord is coming back for a perfect bride, not one filled with deceit, rebellion or one who dishonors Him. At this very moment God is perfecting His church by the Holy Spirit before His return. Many will be left on the outside because of issues in their lives they refuse to deal with.

Thankfully, we have this marvelous provision: *"If we confess our sins, he is faithful and just to forgive us our sins, and to cleanse us from all unrighteousness"* (1 John 1:9). This pardon is available through the precious blood of Christ.

Every day you are faced with dozens of decisions. God is asking you to do what is honorable and right!

CHAPTER 15

GOD'S BEST "IN THE FLESH"

Hollywood awards its Oscars, boxing has its world champion, hotels have their five-star ratings and the fashion industry crowns its most beautiful, but in God's sight there is only one "best."

Into an earth filled with sin and strife, the Father sent the ultimate sacrifice. It was not a sheep or goat to be placed on an altar; He sent the best He had—His only Son.

He did not offer Mohammad, Buddha, Moses or Peter. He gave Jesus, the Son of the living God. This is explained in perhaps the most powerful verse in the New Testament: *"For God so loved the world, that he gave his only begotten Son, that whosoever believeth in him should not perish, but have everlasting life"* (John 3:16 KJV).

Don't overlook the phrase "His only begotten Son."

There was only *one*. Certainly, there have been many great men and women of faith, yet they are not the *only* Son of God.

FROM ABOVE

The reason Jesus became God in the flesh is so we could relate to Him—and at the same time have a glimpse of the Father. Jesus told the doubting Pharisees, *"When a man believes in me, he does not believe in me only, but in the one who sent me. When he looks at me, he sees the one who sent me"* (John 12:44-45).

To confirm He truly did come from heaven above and had lived forever with God, Jesus made statements such as: *"I saw Satan fall like lightning from heaven"* (Luke 10:18), and He spoke often of how He came from the Father.

It was difficult for people in Jesus' day to connect with what He was saying because they did not know what it was like to be with God.

He could talk concerning His unity with the Almighty because He had been both in heaven and on earth. As He explained, *"I and the Father are one"* (John 10:30).

"DON'T YOU KNOW ME?"

When Jesus spoke with His disciples about returning to heaven, Philip said, *"Lord show us the Father and that will be enough for us"* (John 14:8).

Jesus answered the disciple, *"Don't you know me, Philip, even after I have been among you such a long time? Anyone who has seen me has seen the Father. How can you say, 'Show us the Father'? Don't you believe that I am in the Father, and that the Father is in me? The words I say to you are not just my own. Rather, it is the Father, living in me, who is doing his work. Believe me when I say that I am in the Father and the Father is in me"* (vv.9-11).

These were bold statements, making it clear that He was God who had come in human form—flesh and bone. Then Jesus announced that after He ascended to heaven, He was going to send the Holy Spirit to earth—to complete the fullness of the Godhead.

A JUDGE?

As the Son of God walked the paths of Judea, there was so much ignorance, people did not understand who the heavenly Father truly was. This is why the Lord declared, *"I have come into the world as a light, so that no one who believes in me should stay in darkness"* (John 12:46).

Because of lack of knowledge, there were those in the Old Testament who had the mistaken idea God was a stern judge in the heavens handing down punishment and causing people harm. Of course, He was not.

From Genesis to Revelation, He is love—and so is His Son.

Jesus declares, *"As for the person who hears my words but does not keep them, I do not judge him. For I did not come to judge the world, but to save it"* (John 12:47).

Does this sound like a vindictive, uncaring Lord?

The only person who needs to worry about judgment is the one who refuses Christ. Jesus declares, *"There is a judge for the one who rejects me and does not accept my words; that very word which I spoke will condemn him at the last day. For I did not speak of my own accord, but the Father who sent me commanded me what to say and how to say it. I know that his command leads to eternal life. So whatever I say is just what the Father has told me to say"* (vv.48-50).

THE SECOND ADAM

Since man did not understand God's methods or plans, the Father Himself, in the form of His Son, came to earth to show us the way. Jesus actually "lived out" the godly life so we would have an example.

God knew we needed a divine Hero, a Savior, the Anointed One—the Messiah.

He is the One who was promised to Adam and Eve at the fall of man, the One who would bruise Satan's head and take back the authority God had given us (Genesis 3:15). Man had rejected and put aside this power by going against the commandments of God.

Jesus, the Second Adam, came to restore and to make things fresh and new. *"For as in Adam all die, even so in Christ shall all be made alive"* (1 Corinthians 15:22).

The Son of God represented a *living* way through His body which was given for us on the cross and through His blood that was shed for our sin we inherited from Adam.

INTERNAL COVENANTS

The words of Jesus are *"...spirit, and they are life"* (John 6:63). They are birthed by the Holy Spirit of God, and they will produce not only life in the hearer but also the ability to have faith. Remember, *"Faith comes by hearing, and hearing by the Word of God"* (Romans 10:17 KJV).

In the Old Testament the people had the commandments carved on stone tablets, but the Son of God came to place them in our hearts. No longer are they external laws; they are internal covenants based on love.

The Lord is telling us, "I am not way out there in the cosmos on Neptune, Pluto or somewhere over the rainbow. I'm right here in your midst—and I will never leave you or forsake you."

A New Creation

The reason Christ has the quality and excellence of God is because He was with the Father before creation. *"In the beginning was the Word, and the Word was with God, and the Word was God. He was with God in the beginning"* (John 1:1-2). Then, when Jesus came to earth, *"The Word became flesh and made his dwelling among us"* (v.14).

The Person we worship today is not the physical Jesus who walked the earth. He has risen (Luke 24:34) and sits at the right hand of the Father (Mark 16:19) in His glorified body (Philippians 3:21).

When you say "Jesus Christ is my Lord," at that precise moment, the life and the salvation of God flows into you. The old passes away and there is a fresh start. As a new creation, you are righteous, full of peace and joy in the Holy Ghost, and the good workmanship of God.

The Word declares, *"Yet to all who received him, to those who believed in his name, he gave the right to become children of God—children born not of natural descent, nor of human decision or a husband's will, but born of God"* (John 1:12).

An Incorruptible Seed

Once you carry the title "born again," you are

different—a royal priesthood, a chosen generation, a set-apart people, that you might live to the praise of God's glory.

Nothing will ever exceed or be greater than what God has already done for you in Jesus Christ.

A farmer will tell you of the hard work involved to prepare a field for planting. But through the new birth, God has given us an incorruptible seed of God in Jesus Christ.

Mary was a carrier of this eternal life, but the blood type is not determined by the mother; it is determined by the father. The heavenly Father was the Creator Himself and Jesus was born by the Holy Spirit. God's life flowed through His veins.

YOU HAVE FOUND THE BEST

The moment you receive Jesus as your Lord and Savior, the life of God enters your being so you are born again with this incorruptible seed which will never pass away.

This divine life is germinating within and the law of health and blessing from God is working *in* you—forming you into the image of Christ.

Just as Jesus trod the earth, God is walking this world

in and *through* you, not limited by any constraints. Everything God desires, you are able to do through Christ. He still stands on this promise: *"You may ask me for anything in my name, and I will do it"* (John 14:14).

Why continue searching for anything better when you have already found God's best?

Jesus is telling you today, "Go in My authority, glory and excellence."

CHAPTER 16

A MATTER OF PRIORITIES

I f we have not made the Lord Number One, we have likely replaced Him with an idol.

I'm not referring to a carved icon or a golden image of a happy guy with a big belly! No, an idol is anything we have placed on the throne of our lives other than the Lord—the One who gave Himself for us.

When I am convinced of the importance of a mission, it means I will give it my utmost, come hell or high water. I do what I believe is important to God and make it my priority. As a result, according to the promises of the Word, all heaven is mine.

Remember, God declares, *"He shall call upon me, and I will answer him: I will be with him in trouble; I will deliver him, and honor him. With long life will I satisfy him, and show him my salvation"* (Psalms 91:15-16).

When the Word declares, "Thus saith the Lord

Almighty," it means He will do exactly what He
declares.

THE KEYS TO BLESSING

I ask the Lord what He desires or what is pleasing to
Him and He points me to passages in Scripture which
tell me I will be blessed if I specifically do what He
demands. Here are a few of God's priorities:

- *"Blessed is the man who does not walk in the
  counsel of the wicked or stand in the way of
  sinners"* (Psalm 1:1).
- *"Blessed is the man...in whose spirit is no
  deceit"* (Psalm 32:2).
- *"Blessed is the man who makes the Lord his
  trust, who does not look to the proud, to
  those who turn aside to false gods"* (Psalm
  40:4).
- *"Blessed is the man who fears the Lord, who
  finds great delight in his commands"* (Psalm
  112:1).
- *"... blessed is the man who trusts in the Lord,
  whose confidence is in him"* (Jeremiah
  17:7).
- *"Blessed is he who comes in the name of the
  Lord!"* (Matthew 21:9).
- *"Blessed is the man who perseveres under
  trial, because when he has stood the test, he*

will receive the crown of life that God has promised to those who love him" (James 1:12).

■ *"Blessed is he who keeps the words of the prophecy in this book"* (Revelation 22:7).

YOUR FIRST LOVE

People verbally profess to put God first, but do they really love the Lord more than their personal goals, possessions or family members?

The Lord says, *"Return to me, and I will return to you"* (Malachi 3:7).

Do you remember the depth of emotion when you asked Christ to be your Savior?

Well, it's time to go back to your *"first love"* (Revelation 2:4). Then watch what the Lord will do for you spiritually, mentally, physically, financially, and in your relationships.

If we continue to love ourselves more than God, we will remain on a downward spiral, because: *"God opposes the proud but gives grace to the humble"* (James 4:6)—the ones who submit themselves to Him.

HOW BLESSINGS PERPETUATE

In truth, we are dealing with the first two of the ten

commandments: (1) *"You shall have no other gods before me"* (Exodus 20:3) and (2) *"You shall not make for yourself an idol in the form of anything in heaven above or on the earth beneath or in the waters below"* (v.4).

When our priorities are in order, then God sets everything else in place.

In our early years we become educated, yet not necessarily in the things of the Lord. God says we must take His commands to our hearts and impart them to our children, and their children's children. This is how His blessings perpetuate.

HE MADE IT PERSONAL

The Lord of the Universe, who created everything with a single word, says He loves you. God *revealed* Himself through Jesus. He did not just say "I'm in love with you" from the heavens, He spoke those words as a Man on earth.

Was there ever a time in your existence when you fell in love but you never told the person—and that person moved into a relationship with someone else?

God did not allow this to happen. He spread abroad the Good News of His love:

- He took action by making Himself a body—The Son of God.
- He gave Himself a name— Jesus.

- He lived a life to show how the Father loves us, and then gave Himself for us.
- He died on the cross to save and to make us right with God.
- He rose from the dead so we could know what to look forward to— a new life with the Father forever more.

AN ETERNAL LOVE

Those who receive Jesus are given the power to become the sons and daughters of the Most High God (John 1:12).

When we accept His gift of salvation, we are saying, "I love You" back to the Lord. "Thank You for all You have done for me."

Oh, what the Giver of Life has in store. As Jesus says, *"If you, then, though you are evil, know how to give good gifts to your children, how much more will your Father in heaven give good gifts to those who ask him!"* (Matthew 7:11).

When we say, "Jesus Christ, You are my Lord," we are saying we are freely giving Him the right to our lives—with conviction of heart and faith. We trust He will do what He says because He loves us with an eternal love that never dims.

A LEAP OF FAITH

Trust is extremely difficult for those who have experienced heartbreak. They are reticent and not sure if people are really going to be there for them. Who can they trust?

By the authority of the Word, I can assure you that your Heavenly Father will never let you down. *"God is not a man, that he should lie, nor a son of man, that he should change his mind. Does he speak and then not act? Does he promise and not fulfill?"* (Numbers 23:19).

Take a leap of faith and do what the Lord asks.

Believe on Him because He will cherish, respect, honor and love you in return.

WISDOM AND UNDERSTANDING

Let me encourage you to read a portion of Proverbs and Ecclesiastes on a daily basis. It gives us guidance and tells us how to use God's wisdom and understanding in dealing with life situations.

I have read these two books of the Bible since I was a boy of eight or nine years old, and it has protected me from many problems.

The words gave me a conviction of faith to live God's way—to be willing to have courage and stand on principle when those around me tried to lead me into behavior not pleasing to the Lord.

"CAN I TRUST MYSELF?"

The moment you come out of your mother's warm womb, you experience a cold shock. It's just the first of a number of points of trauma during your days on earth. You will experience emotional upheaval every time there is a major change during your journey.

It also happens when we deal with people who betray our confidence. There may even be times when you ask, "Can I even trust *myself?*

But when you say, "Jesus, you are my Lord," you are telling Him you are thankful to have Him in charge of all you do.

The world shouts, "Be your own boss. Run you own life," but that is foolish. The Lord of the universe knows exactly how to direct everything He created—including you. Trusting in His care is the only path to personal contentment and happiness.

" I FIND NO FAULT"

Bury the mistakes of yesterday. Why go through pain, suffering, heartache and heartbreak if you don't have to? You cannot retrace your steps, but you can start over again right now.

God is able to give you a new beginning and lift you from any sorrows you may have experienced.

With open arms, the Lord invites you and says, "Welcome. I find no fault with you and am thrilled you are here!"

NEW PRIORITIES

During my seminary days, the Lord appeared in my room one night. I will never forget that moment.

He began writing a list of the top ten priorities in my life. It was just like I was watching it on the silver screen — one, two, three.

The list showed all of the activities I was doing for God, but He Himself was number seven on the list. Then He gently spoke these words: "Son, I cannot use you the way you are."

Even though I was busily involved in many projects of ministry, He was letting me know that I was controlling the process rather than God doing it through me.

I asked the Lord's forgiveness, and saw our relationship rise to number one. Everything else became secondary.

From that day forward the fire of God burned brightly in my heart and His power began to be manifested.

What about you? Where are your priorities?

CHAPTER 17

HOW EXCELLENT ARE HIS WAYS

T hose who are not aware of spiritual matters have no concept of the work of Satan, so they blame God for every horrendous, painful event that happens in the world—or in their lives.

There are many Christians who have questions concerning how the Almighty works. For example, they do not understand why the Lord would spare one house from fire, whereas another is burned to the ground, or why tragedy might befall a believer, yet a sinner might escape. Yet, Scripture tells us, *"He causes his sun to rise on the evil and the good, and sends rain on the righteous and the unrighteous"* (Matthew 5:45).

Others question why the Lord allows believers to suffer, not stopping to consider it may be to strengthen their faith (1 Peter 1:7) or for spiritual growth (Romans 5:3-5).

The Bible tells us, *"Consider it pure joy, my brothers, whenever you face trials of many kinds, because you know that the testing of your faith develops perseverance"* (James 1:2).

Through every difficulty, the Lord is developing His quality in you.

A PURPOSE—A PLAN

We acknowledge His ways but don't seem to be *certain* of His ways. When things go wrong, many think they have been abandoned by the Lord, yet each step of your journey is for a reason.

Let me assure you that God's will is greater than your will—and He has a purpose and plan for all things.

After many years of ministry I firmly believe you are not going to leave this earth until you have completed what God intends for you to do.

This life is not all there is. Our days are but a speck in eternity. We can compare our lives to an iceberg. What you see on the top is just a portion of what there is. In a similar way, God has given us this moment.

Martyrs for the cause of Christ have died horrendous deaths for their faith, yet their triumph is far greater than their trials. Where are they now? Receiving the crown of their eternal reward.

A "FAITH EXAM"

God sends circumstances for testing and proving. When He told Abraham to sacrifice his son Isaac, it was a great test of faith—even though the Lord knew the outcome in advance.

Abraham was also assured of God's faithfulness. So much so that he before taking Isaac to the place of offering, he said to his servants, "Wait here for us; we will be back."

Then, just as he was about to sacrifice his son, Abraham heard a voice from the thicket say, "Stop! Now I know you believe."

SUFFICIENT GRACE

The Lord is always at work, in ways we often cannot comprehend.

If you are facing a surgery, remember it is not the physician who heals, only God.

He may work through surgeons and doctors at certain times for His purpose to be accomplished, but no man can take credit for anything that God does.

Jesus continues to say, *"...apart from me you can do nothing"* (John 15:5).

The apostle Paul prayed again and again to be delivered from a thorn in the flesh (2 Corinthians 12). This thorn was an angel of Satan sent to buffet him. He prayed, "Lord, take this out of my life."

As you read the accounts of his missionary journeys, everywhere Paul went he was persecuted. But Lord continued to whisper, *"My grace is sufficient for you, for my power is made perfect in weakness"* (2 Corinthians 12:9).

When the apostle heard those words, he was able to say, *"...for Christ's sake, I delight in weaknesses, in insults, in hardships, in persecutions, in difficulties. For when I am weak, then I am strong"* (v.10).

ETERNAL EXCELLENCE

At this very moment, the Lord is working His will through you.

He is shaping, molding, refining and placing the very excellence of heaven in you for His divine purpose.

I pray you will apply the message of this book to your walk with Christ. Remember:

- God Has a quality plan for your future.
- Seek the excellence of God's presence.

- The Lord is your source of justice and mercy.
- Appropriate His wonder working power.
- He promises you will do "greater things."
- The key of honor opens heaven's gates.
- God's love removes all fear.
- Set heavenly priorities.
- Do what is praiseworthy and right.
- Accept God's Son—the best gift ever offered.

The Lord is waiting to pour His eternal excellence and quality into you. I pray you are ready to receive.

FOR A COMPLETE LIST OF BOOKS AND MINISTRY
RESOURCES BY THE AUTHOR, CONTACT:

RANDY C. BRODHAGEN
GLORY TO GOD MINISTRIES INTERNATIONAL
P. O. BOX 4167
PALM SPRINGS, CA 92263

PHONE: 760-321-5222
FAX: 760-321-5773
EMAIL: pastor@glorytogod.org
INTERNET: www.glorytogod.org